AMERICAN TRAGEDY

NOTES

including
- *Life and Background*
- *List of Characters*
- *Critical Commentaries*
- *Character Analyses*
- *Review Questions*
- *Essay Topics*
- *Selected Bibliography*

by
Martin Bucco, Ph.D.
Department of English
Colorado State University

Cliffs Notes

INCORPORATED

LINCOLN, NEBRASKA 68501

Editor

Gary Carey, M.A.
University of Colorado

Consulting Editor

James L. Roberts, Ph.D.
Department of English
University of Nebraska

Cliffs Notes, Inc.   Lincoln, Nebraska

CONTENTS

An American Tragedy Notes

LIFE AND BACKGROUND

Although Theodore Dreiser never received the Nobel Prize for literature, he is recognized today as a genuine American literary pioneer and his massive *An American Tragedy* is acclaimed as one of the most important novels in American literature.

Theodore Dreiser's beginnings were not auspicious. The twelfth of thirteen children, he was born in Terre Haute, Indiana, in 1871. His parents were poor and rootless, and, like Clyde Griffiths, his protagonist-victim, Dreiser spent much of his youth tortured by dreams of girls, wealth, and high society. Also like Clyde Griffiths, he left alone for Chicago, without finishing high school, and worked at odd jobs.

After a year at Indiana University, Dreiser became a reporter for the Chicago *Globe* and hoped to enter the homes of luxury and beauty instead of looking in through their bright windows. He drifted from the *Globe* to other newspapers in the Middle West and finally got a job with the Pittsburgh *Dispatch*. In Pittsburgh he discovered the novels of Balzac.

At the age of twenty-three Dreiser moved to New York, where his brother (Paul Dresser) was a popular songwriter. Here Dreiser began his first novel, *Sister Carrie*, a pioneering work in American literary naturalism. Because of its erotic and moral frankness, its own publishers supressed the book in 1900.

Failing as a journalist in New York, Dreiser next turned to magazines, hoping to treat his assignments more imaginatively than newspapers permitted. By the time his second novel, *Jennie Gerhardt* (1911), was published, he had influential support from such writers as Frank Norris (who had earlier championed *Sister Carrie*), H. G. Wells, and Hugh Walpole.

Dreiser then seriously devoted himself to writing novels. The first two volumes of his "Trilogy of Desire" — *The Financier* (1912) and *The Titan* (1914) — drew a harsh portrait of a ruthless businessman. The *"Genius"* (1915) was a study of the artistic temperament in a materialistic society. In addition, Dreiser wrote stories, plays, essays, and travel sketches. But wide fame and financial success did not come to the leader of the school of American realism until the publication in 1925 of his monumental and controversial *An American Tragedy*.

Dreiser continued to write steadily — stories, poems, travel books, sketches, autobiography, and novels — but none of his works made an impact comparable to *An American Tragedy*. Toward the end of his career Dreiser devoted himself to questions of socialism and religion. His last novel, *The Bulwark* (1946), was published a year after his death and is a Quaker novel of considerable power. Also published posthumously was *The Stoic* (1947), the third and not really finished volume of his "Trilogy of Desire."

INTRODUCTION TO *AN AMERICAN TRAGEDY*

An American Tragedy was published in December, 1925, and issued in two volumes. Dreiser created a poignant yet powerful novel of youthful loneliness in industrial society and of the American mirage that beckons some of the young to disaster.

For years Dreiser had been collecting news accounts about desperate young men who had tried to rid themselves of passing love affairs by violence. The case of Chester Gillette particularly fascinated him. In Herkimer County, New York, in 1906, Gillette lured his pregnant sweetheart, Grace Brown, to Big Moose Lake and drowned her. Discovered and apprehended almost immediately, Gillette was electrocuted at Auburn Penitentiary in March, 1908.

In voluminous detail Dreiser tells the bewildering story of Clyde Griffiths, a son of evangelists, who takes a job as a bellhop, is involved in an automobile accident, escapes to another city, finds work in his uncle's factory, divides his affection between a factory girl and a socialite, entices the pregnant factory girl to a lake, lets her drown, and is himself tried, sentenced, and electrocuted.

For this story Dreiser scrutinized the official court records and the many newspaper reports of the Gillette-Brown case, explored Herkimer County, and inspected Sing Sing, gathering thousands of impressions and details.

The chief tenet of such literary naturalists as Stephen Crane, Frank Norris, Jack London, and Theodore Dreiser is that man is a helpless pawn of his heredity and his environment, a creature caught in the web of causation and chance. Although Clyde has seemingly successful moments, his life is basically one of suffering. Because of his deficient thought and weak will, Clyde is the protagonist-victim not of a "tragic" but of a "pathetic" plot, and in keeping with the naturalistic-pathetic plot, human frailty and futility pervade *An American Tragedy*.

Both the "pathetic" individual and the "tragic" civilization loom large in this novel. In Kansas City, Denver, and San Francisco, we see the Griffithses in a society whose organic community has declined. Clyde's class snobbery is an outgrowth of individualism and urbanization. And we see in Clyde the decline of belief, the growth of the secular ethic, and the fragmentation of his personality.

Although its classic one hundred chapters are divided into three disproportionate books of nineteen, forty-seven, and thirty-four chapters, the ponderous whole is tensely unified. Dreiser's fictional cosmos of indifference toward puny, struggling man reveals the contrast between the weak, the poor, and the ugly and between the relatively strong, rich, and beautiful. Again, he contrasts the photographic world-as-it-is with the visionary world-as-it-might-be. Because of Dreiser's bold contrasts, systematic ambiguity, and uneasy mixture of scientific notions and compassionate feelings, critics often argue whether or not

Dreiser was a "naturalist," a "realist," or an old-fashioned "romantic." Indeed, his descriptions of subjective states compel as much attention as do his documentaries of material surfaces—and both penetrate beneath simple appearance. Aesthetically, his vast network of dramatic contrast makes for fascinating ironies, foreshadowings, and parallels, all of which contribute to the book's unity.

From time to time the reader will note in Dreiser's prose certain crudities and repetitions. Our literary sensibilities might even be offended when, for example, we see Clyde Griffiths "beat a hasty retreat . . ." or when the omniscient narrator informs us that certain emotions "now transformation-wise played over his countenance . . ." or when a young girl wears "two small garnet earrings in her ears" or when a chapter begins: "Yet a thought such as that of the lake, connected as it was with the predicament by which he was being faced, and shrink from it though he might, was not to be dismissed as easily as he desired."

To be sure, most of Dreiser's sentences do not conform to the ideal set forth in, say, Strunk and White's *Elements of Style*. Yet Dreiser's prose on the whole renders the illusion of the ordinary world with extraordinary fidelity. Significantly, claims have been advanced that Theodore Dreiser is one of the world's best worst writers and that he is an impurist with nothing but genius.

LIST OF CHARACTERS

Since nearly two hundred characters appear in *An American Tragedy*, this list includes only the most important.

Clyde Griffiths

The weak but rebellious central character who aspires to wealth, luxury, and beauty—and is electrocuted for murder.

Elvira Griffiths

Clyde's mother, an evangelist who tries to save her son from the electric chair.

Asa Griffiths

Clyde's father, a poor evangelist, who is less effective than Elvira.

Esta Griffiths

Clyde's older sister who runs away with an actor and is left deserted and pregnant.

Oscar Hegglund

A Green-Davidson bellhop who introduces Clyde to worldly delights.

Thomas Ratterer

A friendly Green-Davidson bellhop who later helps Clyde get a job at the Union League Club in Chicago.

Hortense Briggs

A Kansas City shop girl who inveigles Clyde to buy her things.

Willard Sparser

Oscar Hegglund's friend, a show-off and driver of a stolen car in which he, Clyde, and others have an accident.

Samuel Griffiths

Clyde's rich uncle who gives Clyde a job in his shirt and collar factory in Lycurgus, New York.

Gilbert Griffiths

Clyde's resentful cousin who helps manage the factory in Lycurgus.

Myra Griffiths

Clyde's studious cousin who feels compassion for him.

Bella Griffiths

Clyde's socially active cousin who helps Clyde enter Lycurgus society.

Elizabeth Griffiths

Clyde's aunt who invites him to supper.

Walter Dillard

A Lycurgus shop clerk who introduces Clyde to his friends.

Rita Dickerman

A sensuous Lycurgus girl who is attracted to Clyde.

Roberta Alden

A pretty factory girl with whom Clyde has an affair, whose pregnancy and demands of marriage compel Clyde to plot murder and to let her drown.

Sondra Finchley

Clyde's dream girl, a Lycurgus socialite; because of Sondra, Clyde plots to murder Roberta.

Titus Alden

Roberta's poverty stricken father who seeks revenge for his daughter's death.

Orrin Short

A Lycurgus shop clerk from whom Clyde seeks information about an abortionist.

Dr. Glenn

The hypocritical doctor who refuses Roberta an abortion.

Fred Heit

The political coroner of Cataraqui County who first suspects that Roberta's drowning was not accidental.

Orville W. Mason

The vigorous district attorney of Cataraqui County who successfully prosecutes Clyde.

Burton Burleigh

Mason's assistant; he is convinced that Clyde is guilty of first degree murder and he tampers with the evidence.

Alvin Belknap

Clyde's elegant defense lawyer who is retained by Samuel Griffiths.

Reuben Jephson

Belknap's shrewd law partner who concocts an unsuccessful defense for Clyde.

Miller Nicholson

A condemned prisoner who advises Clyde and leaves him his books.

David Waltham

The governor of New York who denies Clyde's commutation of sentence.

The Reverend Duncan McMillan

The kind and sincere young minister who gains Clyde's confidence, believes that he has saved Clyde's soul, but suffers remorse afterward.

Russell Griffiths

Clyde's look-alike nephew, adopted by Asa and Elvira Griffiths.

CRITICAL COMMENTARIES

BOOK I

Chapters 1-5

The first five chapters of this novel depict Clyde Griffiths's fundamentalist upbringing and describe his early jobs. From the beginning, Clyde is uneasy with his situation. Restless and dreamy, he resents his parents's religious work in the mission house and on the city streets. He rebels against his family's poverty and he dreams of escape and material things. Increasingly, he broods on the freedom that his runaway sister gained. Moving from one job to another, Clyde feels lost until he procures a job as a bellhop in a large Kansas City hotel. A new life, a life Clyde has always dreamed about, seems finally possible.

Dreiser bases the conflict between Clyde's paganism and his parents's puritanism on certain theories of Jacques Loeb (1859-1924), an American physiologist. In Chapter 3, for instance, the omniscient narrator elaborates on the idea that materialism or physical matter is the only reality. In this physio-chemical or mechanistic world, physical laws underlie all activity or flux. The individual is trapped in behavior determined by the reaction of his chemistry with outside chemistry. Thus, as a "chemical machine," Esta Griffiths is attracted to another "chemical machine," the magnetic, handsome traveling actor. On this "chemic witchery" or "chemism," declares the narrator, "all the morality or immorality of the world is based." Later, Mrs. Griffiths wonders why the many years of moral instruction and religious training failed her daughter. The answer, according to Dreiser, is that human beings are at the mercy of their biological and environmental determinism—that is, human acts are determined by antecedent causes. As a result of determinism's implying absolute causality, these laws of social Darwinism often tend to make one pessimistic.

Since the characters in this novel do not understand these laws, they view the world as one of accident and chance. Throughout the novel, there is a continual interplay of accident and inevitability, of chance and causality. By "chance," Clyde gets a job at the prestigious Hotel Green-Davidson; Dreiser then employs irony, using images of "dusk" and "walls" to evoke feelings of doom and futility; the "walls", however, appear to Clyde as comprising a dream city, making him feel the possibility of freedom. But it is soon clear that Clyde is unable to compete with the material forces of a deterministic world, a world which is gloomy, loveless, animalistic, fatalistic, and often sordid. In a jungle of predators and prey, Clyde is neither superman nor beast. This, then, is Dreiser's vision of man—a helpless creature in a fierce world whose events are determined by uncontrollable forces.

One of the most important insights in this first section is Mr. and Mrs. Griffiths's inability to understand their son's desires. Ignorantly, they permit Clyde to work in the flamboyant hotel; they are completely unaware of its influence on their son. On the other hand, Elvira Griffiths, although naïve, does react to her daughter's troubles with greater decision than her husband does; Asa Griffiths is a man of meager sensitivity and intelligence. Asa's foil, or opposite, is his brother—Samuel Griffiths of

Lycurgus, New York. Appropriately, Clyde's rich uncle is first presented to the reader through Clyde's vivid, simplistic daydreams — daydreams which usually include some kind of spectacular liberation. Temperamentally akin to his sister, Esta, Clyde yearns for earthly, not heavenly, love. The motion-picture theater and, next door, the drugstore where he works form a glamorous world — a combination of make-believe romance and real ice cream. Clyde, like his parents, is naïve. He is ignorant of his sister's sexual victimization, yet he envisions pagan seductions of his own. His imaginative flights reveal a repressed, unsatisfied life — until he becomes a bellboy. The Hotel Green-Davidson holds promises for Clyde; he has great expectations of independence, expensive clothes, worldly friends, and good times.

Dreiser's method of literary realism, we soon realize, lies in his massive documentation of "things." He spends considerable time and space making inventories of his characters's physical environment. With much factual detail, the narrator delineates the combination mission-home. He even cites, rather cumbersomely, a number of unframed wall mottoes and he describes in detail Clyde's job-hunting and, later, the furnishings of the luxurious Hotel Green-Davidson.

In order to unify this massive, sprawling novel, Dreiser often inserts foreshadowing. Early scenes often anticipate or form variations on later ones. Dreiser's technique, it should be pointed out, is akin to his theory of natural law and material limitations. The language and situations, for example, of Chapter 1 correspond to the "Souvenir" section in the novel's last chapter. The mottoes in the dreary Kansas City mission point not only to Clyde's transgressions, but they duplicate the mottoes in the dreary San Francisco mission; in addition, the evils-of-drink mottoes foreshadow one of Clyde's early transgressions. Other elements point to later developments: Clyde's daydreaming about obtaining help from his rich uncle, Elvira Griffiths's talents for organizing and speaking, and Clyde's desire to drive around with pretty girls. As Esta responds to the traveling actor, so later will Roberta Alden respond to the role-playing Clyde.

As Mrs. Griffiths protects her daughter here, so later she will try to protect her son. Clyde's work as a newsboy anticipates his later notoriety in the newspapers. His work in a department store basement presages his first duty in the shrinking room of his uncle's shirt and collar factory. His work in a drugstore is a kind of prelude to his later inquiries about an aborticide for Roberta. Clyde's secret theater-going is an early foundation for his increasing deception and yearning. An oasis in Clyde's evangelical desert, the sparkling drugstore atmosphere is a small-scale version of the Hotel Green-Davidson, which, in turn, foreshadows the glamour of Lycurgus society. And as the drugstore manager tries to maintain his status by keeping Clyde ignorant, so later will Clyde's cousin, Gilbert Griffiths, do something similar. While retaining his job at the drugstore, Clyde prospects for a better one; later he is reluctant to give up Roberta Alden before securing Sondra Finchley. His standing in front of the Green-Davidson at night, enchanted by its food, lights, cars, and music, prefigures his gazing in awe at the mansions of the Lycurgus wealthy. And as no flirting or fraternizing with the guests is a Green-Davidson rule, so later will this rule apply to Clyde and the factory girls.

Chapters 6-10

These chapters concern sixteen-year-old Clyde's job as a bellboy at the Green-Davidson. For the first time in his life, he has money in his pockets; he can dress well and enjoy himself. Esta's elopement is a great blow to her parents, but, for the first time, life has become exciting for Clyde. More and more, his job provides luxuries. Then in a flashback section, Dreiser describes Clyde's nervous first days at the hotel, when he was making friends with the other bellboys and joining them in parties that included liquor and women. This section enables Dreiser to detail the interiors of the big hotel, the elaborate restaurant, and the ornate brothel.

As Clyde's parents are ignorant of hotel life, so is Clyde. Even a hotel guest tells Clyde that she'd permit no son of hers to work there. To stress further the "dangerous" influence on

Clyde's temperament, the narrator inserts a short essay on the temptations inherent in Clyde's job. Clyde's enthusiasm for material things, as an example, is somewhat like the spiritual ecstasy of a religious convert. The gaudy hotel is Clyde's secular temple. His worshipping at the shrine of luxury contrasts sharply with his former life. He views the young people who are partying as though he were looking "through the gates of paradise." This earthly paradise fills Clyde's imagination. Rewards in this new world of music, lights, and luxury are here and now, not in some Christian hereafter. As an outsider, however, Clyde can only view the magic of this new world; he cannot penetrate its inner sanctum.

Note how often military terms are used to describe Clyde's work. He appears before his "immediate supervisor" and has his "new uniform" and "general appearance" approved before he is "inspected" and "marched" into the lobby to perform "service" while the "relieved squad" is "disbanded." Note too that the battlefield metaphors are interspersed with the sense of the hotel's being a boxing arena, each boy leaping into action at the sound of a bell. This is no accident; Dreiser is indeed concerned with battle—the battle within Clyde Griffiths. Clyde sees this striking panorama as an integrated world. Its organization, brisk activity, and rich atmosphere impress him; the wealth which Clyde sees seems as though it were from *The Arabian Nights*. Tritely put, however, "all that glitters is not gold"; this is Dreiser's point. He shows us that all that Clyde worships is nothing more than an illusion. Working in this changing, transient, anonymous environment, Clyde absorbs false values, and to universalize Clyde's yearning for wealth and women, Dreiser makes the other bellboys yearn for the same things. Their chatter is mostly about ball games, dances, automobiles, restaurants, and entertainment. They try to comprehend their economic condition: why should others enjoy luxury? They all want money, lots of it, yet they don't want to appear grasping and greedy. Hegglund tells Clyde that appearance is everything. Despite how a bellboy feels, he must "seem" polite and mechanical. Civilized disinterest must always mask commercial hypocrisy. Clyde flounders in this maze of deception. Too nervous to ask questions, he finds himself in a wrong corridor; later, "chilled" and yet, at the same time, entranced by a prostitute's bosom, he gulps his wine too fast.

Clyde encounters all of these new experiences with a divided heart. Though eager for pleasure, he fears consequences. He dreams of depraved delights, but his religious training makes him doubt and worry. There is always the promise of a great thrill, but there is always a decision as to the wisdom of it all, the permissibility of it. Clyde lies to his simple and trusting mother, foreshadowing his web of lies at the murder trial. With increasing sophistication, he hides his real wages, his hours of work, and his reasons for being able to buy expensive clothes. Dreiser's technique here shows Clyde's state of mind as a chain of pragmatic questions and answers; these build to a symmetry of alternating pros and cons. Finally, Clyde rationalizes in favor of freedom over restraint, adventure over precept, and pleasure over pain. Although he is nervous and shaky in the brothel, Clyde perseveres, fascinated by the gross flesh. Led upstairs by a young prostitute, he rationalizes that she is more refined than the others. (Her directness later contrasts with Hortense's moods and Roberta's inhibitions.)

Clyde's nervousness, in part, is due to his poor education. Because he has so little to draw on, he must solve each problem in isolation and often under pressure. Thus he relies on hunches and vague feelings, and while learning to solve the many new problems he faces, Clyde remembers Hegglund's advice and practices duplicity. Whether ignorant or knowledgeable, he learns to maintain a masklike solemnity.

Clyde's new clothes add to the luster of his new "reflected" glory. He previously felt a thrill of glory from the theater and the drugstore; now he absorbs the sense of money and glamour and glory from the Green-Davidson. The glory of *things* magically transforms him, making him feel glorious. And Hegglund likes Clyde because the young, naïve boy makes Hegglund feel important and sophisticated. Note in the restaurant scene how the milieu of the Green-Davidson has affected the boys. They feel "older, wiser, more important — real men of the world." Ordering drinks amidst the shiny silverware and china, which reflect the lights of the restaurant, Hegglund feels himself a "person," a "master of ceremonies," and Arthur Kinsella is aware of his "present glory." Clyde and his comrades, however, are more like mirrors than lamps; they are mere reflections of a world of illusion, not the young playboys they imagine they are.

Clothes, in particular, impress Clyde and the bellboys. Clyde discerns what youthful clothes can do for an older hotel guest. Self-conscious in his bellboy hat and uniform, he worries that his hat (a foreshadowing) might fall off. He is fascinated by the smart young men and girls in fashionable coats and furs.

Clyde's new world is a combination of greed and charity, cruelty and kindness. Clyde learns about kickbacks, mutualism, and social cannibalism. Once in awhile he must tip the ice-water man and the headwaiter. In turn, the haberdasher tips Clyde for his patronage. The guest declares that the haberdasher is a robber, but that Clyde may keep the change. The agreeable Ratterer helps the innocent Clyde, as does Kinsella; Hegglund explains the process of mutualism. At the day's end, Clyde gives Squires a dollar. With respect to his unfamiliarity with drink and sex, Clyde is both joshed and protected. At the brothel, the clever prostitute exploits Clyde's sympathy for their respective desires.

Unable to perceive in hotel life the destruction foretold by his religious upbringing, Clyde accustoms himself to the "caloric atmosphere." Sex parades by in the form of flappers, rounders, faded beauties, and homosexuals. Clyde envisions himself with the rich, married blonde who has a string of lovers. Dreiser vividly pictures the brothel and its environs. Amidst gilt-framed nudes and semi-nudes and assorted mirrors and velvet-gowned girls, Clyde views the smoking, drinking, dancing, and petting. Although too nervous to dance, he is fascinated by the prostitutes's sensuality and yet he is rather surprised that one in particular is unaggressive and "quite human." His lusty comrades, the prostitute's seeming refinement, and Clyde's innocence and sexual starvation — these are the forces which drive him to illicit intercourse.

Chance again plays a role in these chapters: Clyde feels "lucky" to get the job as a bellboy; his sense of good fortune is especially strong after his first day of anxiety. He hopes that, by chance, the rich blonde will "fall" for him. He feels lucky to have such good friends as his fellow bellboys. But the section ends ironically when the prostitute informs Clyde that she is in the brothel because of "bad luck."

Chapters 11-16

This section is untypical of Dreiser's usual representation of day-to-day reality. Chapter 13, for example, begins with a recapitulation of the Clyde-Hortense relationship and concludes with the Clyde-and-his-mother conundrum. These episodes have a common denominator: Clyde's money—Hortense wanting it for a coat, Mrs. Griffiths wanting it for Esta. Dreiser shifts Esta's story back to the time of Mrs. Griffiths's secret correspondence. Clyde's inability to inquire directly compels him to do some spying. The narration moves in large units of time. Clyde's several sightings of his mother provide Dreiser with several opportunities to describe shabby neighborhoods and to build suspense. This plot of coincidence and mystery finally brings Clyde to his sister's apartment. Deserted, pregnant, and unwed, Esta Griffiths prefigures Roberta Alden.

In contrast to this bleak world, Ratterer's household has no moral direction, dogma, or religious conviction. His values include dancing, cardplaying, and love-making. Unlike Clyde, Ratterer need not lie about such things to his mother. The freedom and social zest here parallel later events in Lycurgus: Louise Ratterer is late; at Samuel Griffiths's home, Gilbert Griffiths is late. Clyde meets Hortense Briggs; at his uncle's home, he meets Sondra Finchley. Here, night play compensates for day work; in Lycurgus, Clyde will compensate at night for his lonely, daily work. Here, the girls teach Clyde dance steps; later, he will teach Roberta. The narrator views the cottage party, which Clyde prefers to the theater, as one of the "ebullitions of the youthful mating season." The sensational dancing, flask-drinking, spooning, quarreling, embracing, and whisperings resemble the pre-brothel festivities. Because of peer pressure, Clyde drinks and, later, makes a date with Hortense. But knowledge of the human condition—of his mother's subterfuges and his sister's plight—brings pain.

Like many persons, Clyde harbors a feeling of superiority. Hegglund and Ratterer detect this and include Clyde in their activities. He is pleased when the folksy hotel guest comments on his uncommonness and when the prostitute comments on his refinement. At the restaurant, he compares himself favorably with the other bellhops. The girls interpret Clyde's shyness as superiority, and he considers even Hortense as a bit vulgar and coarse. But he translates his sense of superiority into terms which Hortense can understand: money. Unlike Ratterer and Hegglund, he would go without a girl friend rather than date one who was not pretty. He doesn't have much money, but he is determined to "buy" the glamour that Hortense radiates; he will not compromise for less than the best now that he has seen the world of the Green-Davidson.

Clyde's mother tries to understand her son's personality change. She is glad of his new sense of assurance, yet she is worried about his companions's influence. Because of Clyde's past deprivations, she knows that it is tempting for him to be selfish with his money. But Mrs. Griffiths needs the money because of her deception. Granted, her deception is for humane reasons, it is still deception of a sort and figures in the web of lies and deception which make up this novel. Note that Clyde extracts a pledge of secrecy from Esta, lying to her and, later, to his mother about the accidental nature of his discovery and about his inability to borrow money from his friends.

Once again, chance enters the scene: Clyde, hoping for sexual favors, spends money on Hortense; at the same time, his mother "just happens" to need extra money. And, "accidentally" observing his mother writing a letter (a rare thing), he also "happens" to see her in a boarding house neighborhood. By chance, his own errands make it impossible for him to follow her, until about a month later when he again sees her. This time she evades him by turning into an apartment building, but Clyde senses that this behavior has something to do with her writing the letter and her need for money. For the present, he arrives at no conclusion. A week later, however, he chances to see Esta, but he loses her in a crowd. Still later, he chances to see his mother again; thus he concludes that she is secretly seeing Esta.

Clyde's deep anxieties are due partly to his moral defiance and partly because of inherent characteristics. Degrading as Clyde's brothel adventure seems, its grossness afterward glows in his mind. Troubled by semi-public sexual gratification, he yearns for his own "pagan" girl. Feeling refined and superior, he also feels shy and uncertain; he is girl-shy and also girl-hungry. Desiring a girl as pretty as the appealing, but crude, Hortense, he feels "adrift upon a chartless sea in an open boat." As a look bewitched Esta, so a look bewitches Clyde. Forgetting Ratterer's warning, Clyde pleads his affection, flatters Hortense with uncalculated honesty, and is pathetically soothed and hypnotized by her lies.

The morality of Clyde's girl friend is connoted by the name Hortense. A poor girl, she uses males for whatever pleasures or clothes she desires. For the love of Hortense, admirers have committed petty theft—just as for the love of Sondra, the frustrated Clyde will consider murder. Unlike Sondra, however, Hortense is crude and greedy; but like her, she is pretty and shallow. She primps and adores her reflection in mirrors and shop windows, and she employs her sensuous mouth and bright eyes coquettishly and melodramatically. Fickle, affecting indifference, she vamps Clyde to squeeze out rivals. She wavers between disliking and liking Clyde, seeing him as exceedingly gauche, yet attractively refined. Still proud, she submits only to men whom she desires or whom she can enslave. She is quick to let Clyde know, subtly, that she will submit sexually only *after* he buys her the beaver coat.

Hortense's sensuality overwhelms Clyde. He desires to possess her alone. He dreams of voluptuous contact with her smooth, rounded body. Her swimming eyes make him love-sick. Her languorous embraces whet his appetite. Clyde's sweet dream of sensuality seems more real, though, than its impending actuality. Hortense flickers before him as if on a movie screen. His dream girl presses against him, but always he awakens. His masochism is a foil for her sadism. As in a dream, she appears on their first date in the glow of arch-lights. Her eyes are like soft black velvet. Clyde's soul is indeed a battlefield. He is torn by lust and by his sympathy for Esta. When Clyde sees his sister and realizes that she is pregnant, deserted, and unmarried, he finally realizes the extent of his mother's shame. He understands her willingness to lie in order to protect Esta and the other children. He recalls the girl who was deserted in the hotel. And so, although drawn to Hortense, Clyde sees how readily *she* could desert him and his dreams. In fact, she chatters endlessly about "breaking" dates. Mrs. Griffiths, in her hour of need, asks Clyde if he will desert her. Like the girl in the Green-Davidson, Esta is left penniless and in a strange place. Unaware of the extent of his own infidelity, Clyde ironically thinks of his sister's deserter as a "dog."

Unifying foreshadowings and parallel situations abound in these chapters. The clandestine talk between Clyde and Hortense in the department store foreshadows such talk between Clyde and Roberta in the collar factory. As Ratterer dislikes Hortense, so Gilbert Griffiths dislikes Sondra. As Hortense lies to Clyde, so Clyde lies to Roberta. The correspondence between Mrs. Griffiths and Esta foreshadows the letters between Clyde and Roberta and, later, between Clyde and his mother.

Chapters 17-19

Having never really "traveled," Clyde looks forward to a delightful automobile trip with Hortense and four other couples. At the Wigwam, they can eat, drink, and dance. Symbolic of the Jazz Age, the automobile is fast, easy, fun-geared, and possessed of real and illusory power; en route are drinks, gay banter, and refreshment stops. At the Wigwam, Clyde watches the Dionysian dancing of Hortense and the others. Offsetting these glorious moments, however, are other experiences: the terror of a hit-and-run accident, pursuit, a crack-up in a stolen automobile, flight, and further pursuit.

Clyde's excessive sensibility is slowly beginning to devour him. As with illicit sex, it is not the act itself but the possible consequences that troubles Clyde about riding in Sparser's "borrowed" car. But he is weak and so he succumbs to temptation and delights in the trip. Again the idea of Clyde's soul being a battleground is valuable. Made jealous by Sparser's dancing with Hortense, Clyde grows anxious, then angry. Lamenting his lack of strength, he yields to Hortense. He places himself in agonizing situations, determined not to show his jealousy. Unable, however, to control himself, Clyde accuses Hortense of letting Sparser kiss her. He summons up a trace of courage and tries to leave her, but he is too weak. Her empty, new promises are victorious.

Sex and violence are deftly woven into these final chapters of Book I. Hortense, genial and giddy, snuggles close to Clyde in the automobile. But at the Wigwam, she dances with the rhythmic and sexy Sparser. Worldly-wise, Sparser looks deep into her eyes and she stares back. To placate the angry Clyde, Hortense temptingly purses her sensuous mouth. Dreiser likens the young people to "satyrs and nymphs of an older day." Later, Sparser and Hortense return holding hands and, still later, while playing crack-the-whip, Hortense falls and shows off her legs to a laughing audience. Clyde can barely control himself. He thrills to her promise of yielding to him next week, but cannot understand her attentions to Sparser. On the trip back, he holds her hand and kisses her often—until the series of violent mishaps.

This new world of Clyde Griffiths seems like a fantasy to him; it is exactly that. It is a world of make-believe and illusion. Sparser poses as being more than a farm superintendent's son. Secretly borrowing his father's employer's Packard, Sparser pretends to own the car. Hortense removes her hat in the car, less to accommodate Clyde than to show off her new hair style; her plaster beauty mark and rouge dramatize her true beauty's inaccessibility. On the drive, she senses with pleasure Sparser's designs, and when Clyde realizes her fickleness and dishonesty, he pretends indifference. However, he cannot hide his jealousy and disappointment. Hortense first pretends innocence, but then the sting of truth angers her. Greedy for the beaver coat, she feigns liking Clyde best, but her mind is on Sparser. Later, on the ice, she screams in pretended fear as Sparser and Higby pretend to trip her. Clyde labels her a flirt; she labels him a bore, then masters him with her hurt-little-girl act. Clyde thinks of a new strategy: "If she wanted to lie and pretend, he would have to pretend to believe her." Yet she is able to re-convince Clyde that she will have sex with him—shortly before she throws Sparser a secret look.

And then tragedy, resulting from unethical actions and ignorance. Misfortune results from Sparser's fraudulence. Fearful of the owner's early return, he prudently obtains the car earlier than originally planned, but the appointed day threatens snow. Bad luck slows Sparser's race with time: freight trains, muddy roads, bridges, minor accidents, and heavy traffic. Panic drives him from one accident to another—from the incident involving the little girl to that of the lumber pile. By chance (or poetic justice), Hortense's beautiful face is scraped. Finally, Clyde hopes to escape—"if the fates were only kind."

Self-love and self-interest, it is evident, extinguish fidelity and decency. At the inn, Hortense and Sparser forsake their partners and dance together; playing on the ice, she prefers Sparser to Clyde. Later, Sparser fearfully speeds from the scene of his accident with the little girl. When the automobile crashes, Clyde thinks first of himself and then of Hortense; her face bleeding, Hortense runs directly home. When the others scatter, leaving the injured Sparser and Laura Sipes to the police, Clyde also flees. Crawling into a field, he hopes to desert misery, punishment, and disappointment.

The imagery of winter—a snowy road between white fields, dark woods, wave-like sentinel hills, a scarecrow fluttering in the wind, and a flock of crows—foreshadows death and destruction. Ratterer's concern with returning on time anticipates calamity, while Clyde's romantic view of travel foreshadows his hegira in Book II. The Wigwam is a midwestern version of the eastern resort later in the novel. Here, Clyde quarrels with Hortense;

there, with Roberta. The chaotic game of crack-the-whip on the frozen lake foreshadows the tangled bodies of the impending automobile accident and, much later, the climactic upsetting of the rowboat on Big Bittern Lake. As Sparser flees from the wounded little girl, so later Clyde swims away from the drowning Roberta. The police chase in this section foreshadows the search for Clyde after Roberta's drowning. Both incidents inform the trial. Finally, Clyde heads south and west, directions counter to his destiny, north and east; and, again, after Roberta Alden's drowning, he runs in the same directions, south and west.

BOOK II

Chapters 1-11

This section depicts Clyde's early months in Lycurgus. He begins doing menial work in his uncle's shirt and collar factory. Accented by Gilbert Griffiths's pejorative opinions of his country cousin, Clyde's day-to-day reality unfolds. At a dull church social Clyde falls in with three young pagans. Belatedly, the wealthy Griffiths family invites their poor relative to supper; that evening he fleetingly observes Sondra Finchley. Not long afterward Samuel Griffiths, disturbed by his nephew's toiling in the factory basement, orders Gilbert to give Clyde a better job. Clyde then deserts his trio of friends.

Chapters 1 and 2 of this section are set three years after the close of Book I and include descriptions of the grand Lycurgus home of Samuel Griffiths, a sharp contrast to the opening of Book I. We first see Clyde from the viewpoint of his uncle; returning from a business trip, he relates to his family his encounter with his nephew, a bellhop at the Union League Club in Chicago. Chapter 3 focuses on Clyde, flashing back to his flight from Kansas City, noting his odd jobs, the letters he writes to his mother, and his getting a job at the club. Chapter 4 details Clyde's meeting with his uncle and Samuel Griffiths's talk with Gilbert. Rather quickly, then, Clyde is settled in Lycurgus by the end of the chapter.

Underlying his new appearance in his new setting, however, are the laws of heredity and environment. Forced to make his own way after the Kansas City fiasco, Clyde realizes that his fortune depends on himself and his circumstances. Dreiser's naturalism spotlights the machine slave and the industrial basement. In this systematic jungle we see Gilbert Griffiths (chemically chilling and bristling) awe an underling who, in turn, awes an underling; later, at home, Gilbert is awed by his sister's refusal to accept his estimate of Clyde. Yet their mother, comparing her nephew to her tough son, sees in Gilbert his father's force and her family's aggression. Some "atavistic spur," explains the narrator, accounts for ambition.

Equally deterministic is the interplay of chance and causation. Chance brings Clyde to the Union League Club, where Ratterer happens to be working. When Clyde is most anxious about his future, chance produces his rich uncle — a type of fairy godfather. By chance Ratterer links this guest's name with Clyde's almost mythical uncle. In Lycurgus, Walter Dillard feels as lucky to meet Clyde as Clyde felt to meet his uncle in Chicago. Yet Clyde's anonymous position and his inability to fathom his uncle's intentions cause him to drift toward Rita Dickerman. When the Griffithses' tardy invitation arrives, Clyde chances to be involved with (but uncommitted to) his new friends. He feels lucky to be invited, but not to discover that he has such a sarcastic cousin. Planning a simple family affair, Clyde's aunt is irritated that Bella should arrive, by chance, with Bertine and Sondra. Finally, it is only during a chance tour of his factory that Samuel Griffiths scrutinizes his nephew in the shrinking room — and thus causes his immediate promotion.

Change is effected by the chemistry of charity as well as of hostility. Ratterer good-naturedly jockies Clyde into situations where he can confront his rich uncle. Samuel Griffiths himself wonders if his father long ago treated Asa fairly; thus out of obligation if not restitution to Asa, Samuel Griffiths favors his nephew, but nepotism, he knows, is opposed to the law of necessity. Suspicious of Griffiths's nephew, the sweating laborers in the shrinking room grow jealous of Clyde's "class" and "connection."

Although Dreiser maintained the primacy of idea over method, as a writer he did find those techniques which best extended his naturalistic outlook. Latent in Dreiser's old-fashioned block descriptions of Myra and Bella is our sense of Clyde's being the third in a romantic triangle — but not, as it turns out, with his cousins. The tortured dialogue in Book I between Clyde and Esta about the vices of Kansas City contrasts brilliantly with the gossipy debate between Gilbert and Bella about the virtues of Twelfth Lake, and about Bella's many brother-sister friends. Their father, characteristically conservative, formulates his cautious attitude toward his nephew during the dinner ritual. His wife's carefully worded supper invitation (reproduced) creates within Clyde a chain of questions, with answers alternately positive and negative. When Clyde does come to supper, the author contrives that the Griffiths family — Elizabeth, Samuel, Myra, Gilbert, and Bella — greet him in a novelistically manageable way — that is, one at a time.

The author fuses idea and method by his interplay of philosophical materialism and artistic contrast. During Clyde's wandering around Lycurgus, the narrator describes the depot, the factory section, the business center, the slum area, and the residential preserves. Details of the Griffiths Collar Company abound, particularly the main office, the stamping room, and the shrinking room. In his portrayal of an insipid church social, Dreiser catalogs such names as "Micah Bumpus" and "Maximilian Pick." To Clyde, the stately Griffiths home is an earthly paradise, quite unlike the mission and boarding house atmosphere. Samuel Griffiths sees Clyde as a foil to his brother Asa at the age of twenty-one. Sondra and Bertine (foils to Rita and Zella) see Clyde as more malleable than his foil, the willful Gilbert.

The contrast between Clyde and the other characters and between opposing sensibilities in Clyde himself contributes greatly to the novel's acute irony. Guilt-ridden and self-pitying "Harry Tenet" insists in his letters to his mother that he "just went along," that he deserted the scene of the Kansas City car accident because he is legally blameless — the same reason Clyde offers (Book III) for deserting the scene of the boat accident. (Although Clyde technically did not tell Sparser to drive faster, he did remark: ". . . I wish we could hurry a little!") Though Clyde's cousin—not his uncle—regards him as a menial, Clyde discovers that it is as easy for a Griffiths to kiss a Rita in Lycurgus as it was difficult for a Griffiths to kiss a Hortense in Kansas City; this facile relationship negates his promise to his mother to avoid loose companions. The Griffithses' supper invitation saves Clyde from Rita, whom he finds as unchallenging as Sondra finds him. And finding the ragged shrinking room employee to be the same neatly dressed nephew who comes to supper, Samuel Griffiths (out of qualms and self-interest) promotes Clyde. Again, the promotion saves Clyde from Rita Dickerman—but not from Roberta Alden!

As in Book I, Dreiser takes considerable pains with his plot and characterization to prepare the reader for unusual events and behavior. If less dense than in Book I, foreshadowing in Book II is nevertheless notable. In this section Gilbert's jealousy of Grant Cranston foreshadows his jealousy of Clyde. The jail-like factory reinforces Dreiser's "wall" imagery; but the purblind Clyde sees in the high walls only energy and material success, as he does in his uncle's walled garden, where cast iron dogs pursue a cast iron stag. (The chase in Clyde's mind is mostly of pretty Lycurgus girls hurrying to and fro.) Significantly, several Lycurgus people nearly mistake Clyde for Gilbert, a device which readies us for Sondra's significant *faux pas*. Unwilling to risk failure in his uncle's employ, Clyde characteristically plays two ends against the middle by partially withdrawing from his pagan companions, who dance to "The Love Boat." Finally, Sondra Finchley (whose father owns the Finchley Electric Sweeper Company) produces an "electrical" effect on Clyde; this modifier and numerous other "electricity" images prepare us for Clyde's tragic end in the electric chair.

Clyde's ultimate nightmare grows out of his characteristic daydreams. Coming of age, he yearns to become "somebody"; he looks for idols. Samuel Griffiths is pleased by his nephew's idea of him—the hero of an American success story. Clyde even views his authoritative and efficient cousin as some sort of ideal. He realizes how much he looks like Gilbert – but is not Gilbert. Unfortunately, his expectations in Lycurgus exceed his role. When he gazes at his uncle's home and at the pretty girls in the streets, he falls into a mood of enchantment. Savoring his kinship with the Griffithses, he dreams of the future and, growing nostalgic, feels that he could manage even Hortense now. Unable to discern his aunt's supper invitation as simply a "duty," he further daydreams of the Griffithses' wonderful private lives. While Gilbert is jealous of his cousin's good looks, Clyde envies his cousin's power. After the evening with the Griffithses, Clyde daydreams of a love affair with a society girl like Sondra Finchley. Again, his promotion triggers daydreams; he sees himself as reserved, able, energetic.

Clyde's daydreams, however, have an element of pain. Even in Lycurgus, Clyde confronts experience (as he confronted his uncle in Chicago) with a divided heart. He aspires to Union League conservatism, yet regrets that, unlike the Green-Davidson, it is an "Eveless Paradise." Though his opportunity thrills him, his past haunts him. Disliking Gilbert, Clyde nevertheless tries to ingratiate himself to his cousin. Lonely and flattered, Clyde befriends three middle-class exhibitionists, but wonders if this is not another of his mistakes. He grows·to like Lycurgus, but he dislikes his job in the shrinking room and the kinds of people who stay at the boarding house. Dubious, he responds to Rita's "electron" body and debates with himself about continuing the alliance. He strives to overcome his anxiety at the Griffithses' supper. Gazing on Sondra, Clyde desires two contradictory things: to close his eyes completely and to stare at her constantly.

Although he broods outside the Lycurgus *beau monde,* Clyde senses very early that the other employees pay him homage simply because he is a Griffiths. He gains additional respect by exploiting their confusion as to his status. Since the shrinking room workers are below his station, Clyde is civil without pretending to adjust to their sub-bellhop mentality. Instinctively, he maintains a professional distance from Dillard, an attitude which increases the petty clerk's respect. Although pleased by his effect on the girls at the church social, Clyde holds himself as aloof as possible. He summons up enough courage at the supper to suggest to his uncle that he is destined for something better than the shrinking room. Until his promotion Clyde feels that his uncle has deserted him; yet Clyde himself deserts Dillard and the girls soon afterward.

In spite of his sense of superiority among his co-workers, Clyde's soul (like Analschar's in *The Arabian Nights*) is destined not to grow. In flatly saying, however, that the "brainless" Dillard lacks Clyde's "discrimination about the governing facts of life," the narrator contradicts his many efforts to convince us of Clyde's mental fuzziness and analytical impotence. Always Clyde blames his poor performance on his poor education. Gilbert's condescension confuses and frightens him. Among the Lycurgus Griffithses, he often feels that he is a "nobody," and amidst monied females, Clyde often feels inadequate.

Our sense of Clyde as an outsider is strong as he explores Lycurgus, bends to Gilbert's will, and gazes on the Griffiths's mansion. Almost like a trespasser he enters his uncle's iron gates and seats himself at a respectful distance from his aristocratic aunt; from afar, he envies Gilbert's airs. Understanding her son's resentment toward Clyde, Elizabeth Griffiths adroitly reinforces Clyde's role as a social outsider when she informs Bertine and Sondra that her husband's generosity alone brings his poor relative here. From Sondra, Clyde feels destined to win not even a glance.

Some form of inadequacy accounts for most of the pretense in this section. Anxious to impress his uncle, Clyde exaggerates, giving the impression that his father is in religious work *and* the hotel business. Clyde plays to his uncle's pride in himself. From the beginning, Gilbert deceives Clyde: he pretends that he alone decides his cousin's fate at the factory, for his aim is to make Clyde unimportant to his father, his family, and his personnel; since he fears to oppose his father's directives, Gilbert's tools are indifference, omission, and innuendo. Conversely, the sycophantic Dillard identifies with Clyde and garnishes his own petty history. Zella and Rita arrive at the church social "fashionably late" and with demure poise. Bertine Cranston, too, is affected and sly.

However extrinsic, names and clothes reflect a wide spectrum of value. Dillard and his relatives bask in the glory of Clyde's "left-handed connection" with one of Lycurgus's leading families. Proud of his name, status, and status symbols, Samuel Griffiths wishes that Clyde had more commercial acumen and energy, but his nephew's toiling in an undershirt, old trousers, and canvas shoes reflects no glory whatsoever on the name of Griffiths. This prince-and-the-pauper motif is apparent. On the one hand, Gilbert's clothes—his patterned gray office suit, motor coat, leather cap, and gauntlets—impress Clyde; on the other hand, Clyde's poorly cut suit, vulgar tie, and pink-striped shirt disgust Gilbert. But Clyde comes to supper in a tuxedo, patent leather shoes, and a white muffler. Unlike Zella's revelatory scarlet throat ribbon, garnet earrings, and tight black blouse, Sondra's tailored suit, travel coat, and leather accessories enchant Clyde.

To Clyde, Sondra Finchley is the brightest star in Lycurgus's sexual firmament. But his view of her is sacred rather than profane. Until he gazed on Sondra, that lesser sun goddess Rita Dickerman could melt him in her beams. Her furry voice and swaying body could intrigue and intoxicate him. But her rank availability simultaneously attracted and repulsed him. Upon receiving his promotion, Clyde resolves to curb his "abnormal" interests, especially since the factory girls are taboo, remote, and inconsequential.

Chapters 12-22

This section details Clyde's love affair with Roberta Alden. Resolving to make good as a supervisor, Clyde nevertheless is attracted to a newly hired girl. After accidentally meeting at a lake one Sunday, the two conspire to meet again. In time, his desire and persuasion win over her desire and scruples; they meet secretly in her room.

Like Clyde, the other workers are (according to Dreiser) in the grip of a mechanistic universe. In spite of Clyde's elevated status, sexual chemistry and physical beauty inflame him. Sensual employees and summer afternoons arouse his dream life and disturb his managerial equanimity. Roberta Alden is more charming (yet no less vigorous) than the foreign-born temptresses, and like Clyde, she is sexually stirred. Though tolerant of foreign mores, Roberta herself is controlled by her situation, shyness, religion, and morality; in time, however, her sexual chemistry compels her — by chance — to abandon herself to Clyde.

Chance and causality interplay in other ways. Economic need first forces Roberta to work in a factory. Its closing forces her to find work in Lycurgus. The Griffithses' busy summertime social life excludes Clyde and so he turns to Roberta. Her improbable appearance on the shore of Crum Lake at the moment Clyde is daydreaming about her — and she about him — is salvaged from obvious contrivance by their expressed joy in this magical coincidence; but less artful is the expedient manifestation of the boarding house electrician who offers Roberta and Grace a ride back to town. Dreiser strongly *causes* his lovers to meet secretly in Roberta's room through the realism of fall weather, the Griffithses' remoteness and mutual lust.

In spite of Dreiser's documentary method of literary realism, he sometimes impregnates several details with symbolic imagery and develops his story through patterns of association. Besides detailing manufacturing processes, efficiency practices, industrial sensuality, rural poverty, a floral parade, and an excruciating battle between the sexes, Dreiser in one scene simply shows Clyde waiting for Roberta against a backdrop of phallic corn; Dreiser suggests rather than shows sexual abandon, thus reducing possible reader shock and alienation. But Dreiser's more complex treatment of Starlight Park is symbolic of mechanistic determinism: people on a grinding merry-go-round, people captive in swinging aeroplanes, people suspended in ferriswheel cages; below are people in boats, and on shore is a caged bear. The opening of Chapter 16 varies chronological sequence by flashing back (from Roberta's point of view) to events following her canoe ride with Clyde; similarly, Chapter 18 flashes back to the evening after the ride and renders Roberta's reactions to Grace Marr's inquisitiveness.

"Plantings" in this section foreshadow Roberta's drowning: Sondra in a floral parade canoe, Clyde and Roberta in the Crum Lake canoe, Roberta's inability to boat or swim, and the boating incident at Starlight Park.

Dramatic irony surfaces in several places. As Gilbert interviewed Clyde, here Clyde interviews Roberta. Polish Mary's dilemma—to love or lose—parallels Hortense's earlier problem and Roberta's approaching one. At Crum Lake, Clyde reassures Roberta that the canoe is safe, almost as ironic as his remark that on seeing her he "almost fell out of the boat." As sundry girls taught Clyde to dance, in this section he teaches Roberta. After kissing her, Clyde feels that life has given him everything, but when he dances with her later, Sondra is on his mind. That Roberta envisions Clyde's parents as less strict than hers is ironic, as is her conviction that once she yields to Clyde they will never again quarrel.

Aesthetic tension as well as irony rises out of several noteworthy contrasts. We first see Clyde alone on Crum Lake, very much apart from merry couples in other boats. Roberta's boarding house compares unfavorably with the homes of the wealthy, but both at first are beyond Clyde's reach. Compared to the calculating Hortense and the indiscriminate Rita, Roberta is pleasing, but Clyde wonders if she will become like Hortense, wily and evasive. Unlike the Newtons's, the Gilpins's boarding house standards are relaxed. By the end of this section, the day-night contrast is pronounced—routine and craving in the factory as opposed to amour and fulfillment in Roberta's room. Clyde realizes his dream of sexual conquest.

Let us examine the pattern of dreams in this section. As head of a department, Clyde visualizes a sense of the whole factory. Alone on Crum Lake he daydreams of resorts, dancing, racing, and boating with Sondra Finchley, but then he falls to daydreaming about Miss Alden, someone he would never marry but someone physically closer to him now than Miss Finchley. Still an outsider, he senses the height of his ambition and the depth of his sensuality. As if still dreaming, he sees Roberta at Crum Lake. As Sondra floated past Clyde in her floral canoe, so here Clyde floats toward Roberta. Like Clyde, she dreams of a better life — training, freedom, fun. To Roberta, Clyde moves from his superior world into her humdrum world and makes her unlighted room into a paradise; after his sexual exhaustion, however, the fickle Clyde imagines Sondra and her society.

Both Clyde and Roberta have divided minds and mixed emotions. At the floral parade Clyde is deliciously pained. At Crum Lake his pageant of the bleeding heart is overwhelmed by loneliness. Roberta fears and desires to join Clyde in the canoe. Later she feels her clandestine meetings with Clyde are disgraceful, but precious. Recalling his sad experiences with Hortense, Clyde decisively shuns Roberta until she surrenders. Suffering from a paralysis of opposing forces, she finally consents to their intrigue and is daily pained for her nightly pleasure.

At this point Clyde is above pain and still riding on the crest of his pleasurable sense of superiority. Seeing himself as a figure of some consequence, Clyde early displays indifference to the factory temptresses, especially the heavy and the unintelligent; but he wonders perhaps if Roberta has more potential than merely doing factory work. Forced to work in a factory when she was young, Roberta has always been thought of as a "factory type" — and has thus become conditioned to her station — far below the nephew of Samuel Griffiths. Bending Roberta to his will, Clyde persuades her to meet, to kiss, to dance, and to let him into her room. After his conquest, Clyde regards himself in the mirror as a Don Juan or Lothario, a lover well above the station of his mistress.

Like Clyde, Roberta became convinced early in life that family poverty discourages attractive lovers. She respects the taboo that factory girls should show no romantic interest in supervisors. Since even the churchly are standoffish to Roberta and Grace, the girls find no diversion or entertainment in Lycurgus. So high does Roberta hold Clyde that she fears her interest in him is not legitimate. Clyde's eagerness for secret liaisons reduces Roberta to a backstairs mistress whom he could desert at any time.

The theme of desertion is important here. Having marooned Clyde in a small official position, the Griffithses proceed to dismiss him. In turn, Clyde moves to a better boarding house and drops Dillard and the girls. He learns that the factory system hires workers and then fires them (or those less efficient) just as freely. Because of Clyde, Roberta bolts from her friendship with Grace Marr. Although Clyde never suggests marriage, Roberta feels secure that he never will forsake her.

But the reader knows more of Clyde's desertions and deceptions than does Roberta, who is herself (like most of Dreiser's characters) capable of "wrongdoing." For example, Clyde attends church for social rather than religious reasons. In and out of the factory, he schemes with Roberta. To meet Clyde secretly, Roberta lies to the Newtons and to Grace. Her route to trysting places is circuitous. Caught in one lie, Roberta moves from the Newtons to the Gilpins. Clyde is well aware that his intentions toward Roberta are not honorable. To make Roberta jealous, he flirts with other girls in the stamping room. Finally, on his "left-handed honeymoon" Clyde is conscious of his seduction of the innocent and of his spiritual betrayal.

Here again, clothes symbolize victory and defeat. Sondra's Indian parade outfit captures Clyde's romantic fancy. In spite of Roberta's old brown hat, commonplace suit, and sensible shoes, Clyde discerns Roberta's sweetness, but fancies how much sweeter she would look in smart clothes. At the factory one of the foreign girls, Ruza, admires Clyde's polished shoes and bright buckle, and at Crum Lake, Roberta admires his pale blue shirt open at the neck; the sartorial details which Ruza notices reflect Clyde's past Kansas City glitter, while those which Roberta notices are symbolic of Clyde's future—his electrocution in a shirt "open at the neck."

Chapters 23-33

This section focuses on Clyde's love for Sondra and his dis-
enchantment with Roberta. After accidentally meeting Clyde
one evening, Sondra is so charmed by his attention and so an-
noyed by Gilbert's indifference that she arranges for Clyde to be
invited into her social circle. Much to Gilbert's disgust, his
cousin's growing popularity forces the Griffithses to receive him
socially. Roberta spends part of the Christmas holidays on her
family's drab farm, while Clyde anxiously awaits participating in
the activities of the wealthy. Breaking engagements with
Roberta, the enamored Clyde dreams of marrying Sondra and of
gaining wealth and position. Roberta then discovers that she is
pregnant.

As causation and chance determine Roberta's pregnancy, so
these forces shape other lines of action. The narrator's reference
early in this section to a happening destined to bring about an
unforeseen chain of events is Sondra's mistaking Clyde for his
cousin. Social invitations follow, and conscious of public rela-
tions, the Griffithses are forced to treat Clyde like they do their
friends. Gilbert sees Sondra as the instigator. To Clyde, however,
her "actinic rays" are powerful; Sondra herself cannot fully understand why she is so attracted to Clyde. Meanwhile, the frustrated Roberta wishes that she'd had "a chance like some girls."

Dreiser delineates at length those events bringing Clyde
into Sondra's circle. Featured are such things as conformity,
rumor, and revenge. Again, in the mass of detail we detect symbolism. Symbolism appears in Dreiser's bird and sun imagery.
At the Trumbull party, one young socialite looks down on Clyde
"as a spring rooster might look down on a sparrow." But Sondra
is Clyde's sweet bird of happiness; at the party Miss Finchley is
indeed finch-like, "tripping here and there in a filmy chiffon
dance frock shaded from palest yellow to deepest orange." And
as a sun goddess, her temperament requires the free flow of
Clyde's adulation. Meanwhile, Roberta's mood in Biltz is sug-
gested in a bleak scene of gray twigs, rustling leaf, and wrecked
outbuildings. The opening of Chapter 30 balances our antipathy

for Clyde against our sympathy for him. The scene in which Roberta waits for Clyde flashes to one when Gilbert is angered to see Clyde's name in the society news. Dreiser reproduces four key documents in this section: the invitation to Jill Trumbull's dance (with Sondra's notation to Clyde); Clyde's note of excuse to Roberta; the Lycurgus *Star* item concerning Vanda Steele's party and the upcoming New Year's Eve party in Schenectady; and Roberta's hysterical note to Clyde after she discovers that she is pregnant.

Dreiser's parallels and contrasts are lucid. Sondra sees Clyde as Gilbert's direct opposite. The narrator sees Sondra as a refined Hortense Briggs. Clyde sees Sondra as superior to Roberta, but Roberta as superior to Bertine Cranston. Clyde's partygoing reads like passages from an Ivy League novel of manners, while Roberta's homecoming sounds like a chapter from a gloomy midwestern farm novel. The land-bound Titus Alden, like the city-bound Asa Griffiths, is a portrait of failure. And like Clyde's sister, his bewildered mistress fears that she might burden (or even destroy) her family.

Throughout this massive novel, devastating irony duplicates life's complex patterns. It is not the Griffithses but their friends who first recognize Clyde socially. Sondra's appeal to Clyde to enter her automobile echoes Clyde's appeal to Roberta to enter his Crum Lake canoe. Both Roberta and Clyde fabricate excuses — she to be with him and he to be with Sondra. Certain details implement important later events: while dancing together at the New Year's Eve party, Clyde and Sondra discuss swimming; at the party, two young men indicate that they work for General Electric Company; and Gilbert surmises that some calamity will befall "one or another of the bunch." And it is only when Clyde and Roberta regard the end of their affair that Roberta discovers that the life in her womb has trapped her.

This section also intensifies our awareness of Clyde's daydreams. On one of his night strolls past opulent homes, he stands vigil before the Finchley residence and projects an Arabian Nights type of yearning. After meeting Sondra again, he dreams of his impending rise. As a reality, Roberta pales; as a dream, Sondra pulls. Sondra is princess to his commoner. Guided by Sondra in this Christmas card world, he feels transported to Paradise. He desires to fondle her as one fondles a perfect object, or as a devotee gazes into the eyes of a saint.

Clyde's yearning does not really puzzle others, but his divided nature does. Below the surface of Clyde's social success runs a deep current of self-distrust. He is unable to interpret his relatives's taciturnity as a sign of irritation or pleasure. Eager and mournful, he puzzles Sondra, who is cautious, dubious, and swayed. Although Clyde wants to break with Roberta, he is too weak and unresourceful. He rationalizes. Torn between social passion for Sondra and sexual passion for Roberta, he is lured by one but returns to the other. Sondra herself has mixed feelings about Clyde's apologetic impetuosity. But in the face of Sondra's diplomatic encouragement, he resents Roberta and justifies his dereliction more and more.

Clyde's lofty opinion of himself is colored by his becoming part of the Lycurgus social scene. Feeling above the commonplace world, he looks in mirrors and slyly enjoys his revenge on Gilbert. He marvels that with so many men surrounding Sondra that she prefers him. He is blind to the real reason why the Griffiths family invites him to Christmas dinner. Sondra lifts him upward while Roberta holds him down, but he smugly tells Roberta one evening that he likes Sondra Finchley only "some."

While showing Clyde's temporary run of social luck, the narrator insists on his protagonist's essential deficiency. Disposed to concern itself with immediate cares, Clyde's temperament is "as fluid and unstable as water." Among the elite he often feels ineffective, doubtful, uneducated. If Sondra Finchley seems at times beyond his grasp, Bertine Cranston seems beyond his comprehension. When Roberta discloses her pregnancy, Clyde feels most inept.

Not Clyde's spiritual poverty, but his material poverty, compels urbane society to decree that Clyde is socially but not matrimonially eligible. Because her love for Clyde overreaches her moral training, Roberta practices duplicity. If caught, she plans to explain that Clyde is a relative and then move on to another boarding house. Similarly, Sondra popularizes Clyde through her friends. Likewise, Clyde conceals Sondra's invitation from Roberta, and should anyone at the Trumbull party ask about his educational background, Clyde is ready to answer that he studied mathematics at the University of Kansas. Misinforming Gertrude Trumbull that he has no girlfriend, he also misinforms her sister Jill that his father manages a Denver hotel and that his uncle proposed his career in Lycurgus. To reach Sondra, Clyde bluffs that he has taken up tennis. Later, to attend the Steele party, Clyde uses his uncle as an excuse to Roberta. Sondra and Clyde agree to camouflage from others their vibrant mutual attraction. Contrarily, Clyde tries to hide from Roberta his indifference to her; she senses, however, his hypocrisy in regard to her pen-and-pencil gift. In turn, Roberta cloaks her claims on Clyde, but confides, in part, to her mother. Later, Roberta challenges Clyde's story about the Steele party, and Clyde covers one lie with another. In short, he conceals Sondra from Roberta and Roberta from Sondra. Roberta's pregnancy he first views as a lovelorn stratagem.

No longer can Clyde feel lustrous in Roberta's sight; only Sondra's radiance can reflect glory on him. In turn, Sondra feels regal in the adulation of Gilbert's handsome look-alike; Clyde's naïve confession that he searches for her name in the society news captivates her. Ironically, Clyde impresses Sondra's friends less than the fact that *she* is impressed. But to Samuel Griffiths the hospitality her circle extends to Clyde reflects well on the Griffiths name.

Clothes continue to reflect roles. As a man-about-town, Clyde makes new purchases. Gertrude Trumbull notes that Clyde sometimes wears a cap and belted coat similar to Gilbert's. To the Trumbull party Clyde wears a collapsible silk hat and white muffler. There Clyde learns of his cousin's notion that cheap collars have a redeeming social value. The narrator later attributes Sondra's activities to the opportunity it affords for frequent changes of costume. To fascinate Clyde, Sondra comes to the Steele party in a red Spanish shawl.

Initially, Sondra thinks that if her interest in Clyde doesn't succeed, she can drop him without harm to herself. Both she and Clyde break other engagements to attend the Steele party. Gradually Roberta wonders what Clyde's little desertions portend. In Biltz, she herself considers leaving her family before Christmas, for fear that Clyde will abandon her for his society friends. When Clyde meets Roberta late Christmas night, she feels already betrayed.

Chapters 34-47

This section details Clyde's desperation and Roberta's death. The narrative line moves relentlessly forward. Clyde journeys to an out-of-town drugstore, but the aborticide for Roberta proves ineffective. He sends her to an out-of-town physician who turns down her pleas for an abortion. Happening upon the Alden farm one day, Clyde views marriage to Roberta as a dismal ending to all his bright dreams. Clyde declines Roberta's solution of a temporary marriage and hopes to elope at Twelfth Lake with Sondra. After reading a newspaper account of a double drowning, Clyde daydreams of Roberta's death. When she threatens to expose him, he consents to marry her at a lake resort, but plots to cause an "accidental" drowning. Ironically, the boat does capsize accidentally, but Clyde does not answer Roberta's call for help.

Though not seeing himself as a "determined" animal, Clyde yearns for moral freedom and the unencumbered life. Forced to overpay for ineffective pills, he in turn forces Roberta to visit the doctor without him. Necessity causes the emergence of latent shrewdness in Roberta and cunning in Clyde. Meanwhile, the chemistry of love is active between Clyde and Sondra. The narrator ambiguously comments that some people might view Clyde's appearance at the Alden farm as "determined" by an ironic or malicious fate. Rural poverty forces Clyde to discern his life as a pattern of unfulfilled promises, as a horrible series of social abortions. The aborted life theme culminates in the drowning of Roberta and her unborn child at the end of this section and in the execution of Clyde at the end of the next. Clyde's instinct here is to break his aborted career pattern.

In the world of causation and chance, Clyde's problem is to arrange an accident. From a Christian point of view, the devil and original sin possess Clyde; in spite of his scruples, murder forces its way into his mind. At times he seems almost deranged. Pathologically hovering between reason and unreason, he senses the usefulness of lonely Big Bittern. The newspaper item is like a malignant mental jewel, blinding him to alternatives in his drive to join the monied society of Lycurgus. His survival depends on Roberta's death. At Big Bittern, he senses that moment which he — or something — has planned to determine his fate. But his own will to live lashes out against death, murder, mutability. The sequence of events differs from the district attorney's later version. In chemic revulsion, he lashes out, striking Roberta's face with his camera — symbolic of his motion picture dream world. She screams, the boat lurches, and as Clyde apologetically strives to assist her, the left wale of the capsizing boat strikes Roberta's head. She comes up once, stares at Clyde, and screams his name for help.

The death-crying weir-weir and the other birds which Clyde sees and hears in this section ironically underscore Clyde's futile struggle to capture his sweet tennis-playing Sondra, "poised bird-like in flight." Two natural settings symbolize an invitation to death — drought at the Alden farm and drowning at Big Bittern. Impending death by water reverberates not only in Clyde's lakeside photographs of Roberta, but in his damp hands and liquid eyes. But perhaps most metaphorical of all is Dreiser's description of Clyde's thoughts, linking them first to an Arabian Nights genie and then, in tortured rhetoric, to a sealed and silent hall wherein Clyde contemplates the ambiguity of good and evil. Dreiser's clipped, italicized, parenthetical external data impinging on Clyde's mind as he gazes out of the train window represents Clyde's bi-leveled thoughts and varies Clyde's extensive plottings. Information withheld in this tense section comes to the reader in condensed flashbacks: Clyde's hasty telephone declarations to Roberta make sense only after we see him pondering his earlier drive with friends to Big Bittern and the guide's conversation; and on the train to Utica, Clyde recalls how (after his telephone talk with Roberta) he secured tourist folders at the Lycurgus House. While Clyde plots Roberta's death, the ironic narrator reveals Roberta's simultaneous rejuvenescence.

Photographic realism appears in Dreiser's character sketches, epistles and reportage. The thumbnail sketches include a city druggist, a country doctor, an upstate farmer, and a forest guide. Through their letters to Clyde, Dreiser reveals the essential Sondra and Roberta. Sondra's letters are affected and shallow while Roberta's are plain and probing. The misery and defeat of Roberta's letters turn Clyde to the ease and gayety of Sondra's. Thereafter, Roberta's letters become even more urgent, terminating in her shrill threat of exposure. Central to Clyde's machinations is the extended Albany *Times-Union* account of the double drowning in Massachusetts.

Like the journalist that he was, Dreiser notes the unexpected, the shocking contrary. When Clyde procures an aborticide for Roberta, her relief is great, for she "almost" prefers death to disgrace. With Roberta's problem seemingly solved, Clyde sees before him a "glorious dénouement." Again frustrated, he tells Orrin Short that the factory worker seeking an abortionist is poor, timid, and stupid. Unknowingly, the hypocritical doctor, as it were, decrees Roberta's doom by declaring that he cannot destroy embryonic life. Like the iron stag in his uncle's garden, Clyde now feels like "a harried animal, pursued by hunter and hound." While their mothers show anxiety, both Sondra and Roberta scheme to marry Clyde. Sondra's baby talk has an "almost electric if sweetly tormenting effect" on Clyde. As if subconsciously making his declaration of independence from Roberta, Clyde plots murder for the Fourth of July weekend, but then decides *not* to think of murder anymore. Sondra informs Clyde that she never will give him up, and her brother Stuart remarks on the car trip to Big Bittern that "the country up here kills me." Contemplating murder, Clyde asks himself:

"Who would see? Who would hear?"—ironic statements when
we consider the mission house motto: ". . . MY SINS ARE NOT HID
FROM THEE."

As always, Dreiser's foreshadowing forges irony and narrative momentum. Roberta fears that the aborticide is innocuous.
Separate journeys to the abortionist foreshadow separate journeys to the lakes. Whether intentional or not, there is verbal
irony and foreshadowing in the doctor's reply to Roberta's lie
that her husband is a poor electrician: "At least all electricians
charge enough." Roberta's plea for abortion and the doctor's plea
for preservation point to the question of capital punishment in
Book III. The pines that "sentinel" Twelfth Lake foreshadow
Big Bittern. An index to the theme of pursuit, two wolfhounds lie
on the Cranston grass. The automobile ride to Big Bittern prefigures Clyde's taking Roberta there. And in daydreaming of
murder, Clyde also has a nightmarish vision of electrocution.

In fact, more and more Clyde's dreams turn to nightmares.
Realizing the fraility of dreams, he tantalizes himself with the
idea of ruin. Though Roberta's plan of secret marriage is sound,
Clyde fears exposure. Clyde dismisses as melodramatic his
movie dream of a mock marriage to Roberta, but not his vision of
a glowing marriage to Sondra and of his position in the Finchley
Electric Sweeper Company. Roberta hopes that after their baby
is born, Clyde will love her again; Clyde hopes that at Twelfth
Lake he and Sondra can elope. Avoiding the "black cloud" of
Roberta, he pursues his "golden dream" of Sondra. Clyde fears
losing Sondra in a boat accident; but the likelihood, he thinks, of
losing Roberta that way is greater. But to dream of this is like
"committing a crime in his heart." Dantesque nightmares plague
him: a biting black dog, a gloomy place of snakes, and a great
horned beast. Clyde finds Twelfth Lake to be a paradise, but he
awakens to the reality of Roberta. Of the similarity between his
nightmares and the frogs, snakes, and slime of Big Bittern, Clyde
is unconscious. Almost "nebulously," Roberta steps into an
"insubstantial" rowboat on an "ideational" lake. Real world and
dream world fuse. In a "crystal ball" of lake, Clyde sees Roberta
drowning. His soul seems to fly away and a bird cry wakes him
to reality.

In the opening of this section, Roberta's condition tempo-
rarily shocks Clyde into reality, but failure soon drowns his renewed sense of superiority. In obtaining the aborticide, both
Clyde and Roberta are impressed with his luck and efficiency.
But in developing his vein of hardness, he threatens Roberta
with desertion should she expose him. He rationalizes his
superiority: her demands are harsh and she also deserves blame
for their intimacy. The narrator explains that Clyde is an "illusion
of the enormous handicaps imposed by ignorance, youth, poverty, and fear." For his liaison with Roberta, Clyde blames his
folly, weakness, and loneliness. He considers deserting, but
hates the misery of drifting. Wretched and insufficient, he is
assailed by problems too complex and too forceful. In a state of
mental turbulence, he rents a boat. His will and courage fly,
leaving befuddlement and panic. In the end, he sees his "silly
plotting" as "pointless planning."

But until this time, social diversions offer Clyde respite from
his grasping at straws. His infatuation with Sondra diffuses his
concern for Roberta. Into the jaws of his nightmare, he pursues
his dream of Sondra. He rationalizes that Esta survived, that he
could help Roberta financially after he marries Sondra, that
Roberta's death would save her from her own terror, and that
Sondra would be saved from heartache. Although the idea horrifies him, Clyde yearns for an accident. His mind torn and his
emotions riotous, his remorse for Roberta is always temporary.
He tries to balance the possibility of capital punishment against
the loss of Sondra. Subtly overriding all objections, Clyde's dark
genie whispers of the way that Clyde must go. Yet on the train
and on the bus, Clyde is still divided. On the "death pool," he
feels sympathetic hands on his shoulders, but after his vision of
Roberta in the pool, his courage again deserts him. His face
reflects fear and desire, the compulsion to do and *not* to do — to
reach out and save her and *not* to reach out and to let her drown.
The contradiction resolves itself as Clyde listens to the authoritative voice declaring that she cannot save herself, that she might
drown him, that he should rest a moment. As he swims to shore,
Clyde thanks God that he did not kill Roberta — but on shore he
begins to doubt.

In life's storms, Dreiser's frazzled characters throw overboard their moral charts and compasses. Lying to the Starks that he must write a report, Clyde misrepresents himself to the bilking Schenectady druggist as married. For Orrin Short, Clyde fabricates a "troubled" factory worker. Clyde gulls Roberta into believing that the doctor is not young—true, as it turns out—and then insists that she delude the doctor into believing that she is alone, betrayed, penniless. But too proud to tell the doctor that she is deserted, Roberta lies that she is married and poor. When the doctor sees through the deception of "Ruth and Gifford Howard," Roberta then lies that she is single and deserted. Clyde must deceive Sondra in order to accompany Roberta to the doctor a second time, but Roberta discerns that Clyde's habitual excuses are bogus. To marry Roberta now and move to Denver would expose many of his past lies about himself. To gain time, Clyde tells Roberta that he cannot marry her now, that he first must find another job; in turn, Roberta admits to having saved over a hundred dollars. At Twelfth Lake, Sondra pretends that she is unaware of Clyde's arrival, though her mother is suspicious. He further fibs to Sondra about his delay in returning to Twelfth Lake. On their cloak-and-dagger journey to the lakes, Clyde's prevarications are varied and many, but he doubts if he really can accomplish a drowning.

Roberta's lying to the doctor about her sham desertion, Clyde believes, will gain sympathy, protect his name, and cost him less; Roberta believes that Clyde might abandon her. Upon seeing the dismal Alden farm, Clyde considers leaving immediately. Receiving no replies to her letters, Roberta fears that Clyde indeed has left her. Clyde feels more and more that circumstances will force him to forsake everybody and everything. Again he thinks of flight as he plots the murder, but the accident occurs after his courage has failed him. On shore, the delinquent Clyde knows that he refused to rescue Roberta, that he destroyed her by the simple act of desertion. Ironically, Clyde's new straw hat (with the lining ripped out) and Roberta's hat (with the lining intact) reappear at Clyde's trial (Book III) to haunt him.

BOOK III

Chapters 1-9

This section deals with Clyde's flight and capture. The coroner of Cataraqui County receives the "facts" of a double drowning. After Roberta's bruised body is retrieved, the coroner and the district attorney discuss the political advantages of the latter's solving a "murder." As lawmen prepare to track down Clyde after Roberta's letters are discovered in his room, a flashback records Clyde's making his way to the Cranston's lodge and doubting that Roberta's drowning will appear accidental. As Clyde lingers on the beach, the suspenseful chase plot concludes. Fearing exposure before his friends, Clyde confesses to the accident but informs his story with falsehoods.

Suspicions early coalesce into the certainty of foul play. The casual chain begins with Roberta's bruised face and her unmailed letter to her mother. People wonder about the "wife's" body — so light, so bruised — and no "husband's" body or bag left at the inn. Furthermore, "Carl Graham" and "Clifford Golden" appear to be one and the same person. Because of his "psychic sex scar," District Attorney Mason, brooding on the false registrations and on Roberta's beauty, suspects pregnancy and thus orders an autopsy. Mason vows to find the murderer. When Mason suggests to Titus Alden that his daughter might be the victim of wrongdoing and violence, the father's animal instincts, his curiosity, resentment, and love of the chase are aroused. Quoting biblical scripture, Titus pauses in the doorway, "a man expressing in himself all the pathos of helpless humanity in the face of the relentless and inexplicable and indifferent forces of life!" Because of his own early buffetings by chance and by established wealth, Mason clings to his version of the murder: the contempt of a rich and sophisticated youth for a poor farm girl. And thinking of Clyde Griffiths's telephone pseudonym ("Mr. Baker"), Mason realizes the similarity of "Clifford Golden," "Carl Graham," and "Clyde Griffiths." Circumstances point to Clyde Griffiths as being the murderer of Roberta Alden.

The details in Dreiser's protracted causal chain create suspense. Seen by the reader for the first time in Chapter 6 of this section, Clyde seems (during and following his hike and arrival at the Cranston's lodge) mentally deranged. Through surrealistic narration, past events in Clyde's early nightmares and fearful visions mingle with current ones and foreshadow others, including his arrest. Not he — but "something" — killed Roberta for him. The focus shifts back and forth, between Clyde and his pursuers, until unable to run and unable to stay, he lingers and succumbs to the lawmen.

Out of the panorama of tragedy grow many splendid, even comic-relief ironies. For example, Coroner Heit instructs Earl Newcomb to telephone his wife — he might be late; in turn, Newcomb asks Zillah Saunders to telephone his mother — for the same reason. Like Clyde, Mason is looking for a solution to the problem of his future. As the young people sought Titus for directions, so Titus thinks that Mason comes for the same reason. It is highly ironic, of course, that Mason should consider Clyde to be one of the idle rich. Under the peaceful awnings of the comfortable Cranston lodge, Clyde finds little peace or comfort. In the launch to the Casino Golf Club, Sondra dares to stand while the driver deliberately ricochets the boat. Dreiser's omniscient point of view provides us with information inaccessible to Clyde or Mason. Unlike agents of the law, the reader is privy to Clyde's world; unlike Clyde, the reader is privy to the actions of the law. Thus the reader has a great intellectual advantage as he watches Clyde flounder into Mason's trap. This distance enhances Dreiser's trenchant ironic effects — just as irony magnifies the pathos inherent in Mason's thinking that Roberta was seduced, then viciously murdered by Clyde.

In fact, there is no end to emotional projections. At the rambling Cranston lodge, amid the bright lakes, Clyde spends his time alternately dreaming of delight and hope and frightened by shadows and unknown terror. Sondra envisions their romantic opportunities during the impending camping trip — "and once more like a bright-colored bird she was gone." The bright flotilla of canoes on Bear Lake is a manifestation of the floral parade

(Sondra represented a Mohawk Indian legend); the trip also is a manifestation of the Wigwam (where Clyde's Kansas City friends once sought a bright dream). Even Third Deputy Swink has a daydream — to arrest Clyde.

The projection of self-interest springs from man's dual nature. Titus is torn between his grief for his daughter and his desire for revenge. Mason is torn between commiseration for the Aldens and political profit for himself. Clyde's near derangement is an outgrowth of his confusion as to his guilt or innocence. He believes that he did experience a last-minute change of heart, but he does not place that *moment* in the water; conveniently, he places it in the boat — *before* the accident. He uses public incredulity and fear of losing Sondra as rationalizations for his crime-fleeing instinct. Whatever peace of mind he attains through this mental block, he contrarily thinks that had he been calm and civil to the hunters they could not suspect him for "the murderer that he was." He is torn between remaining at the Harriets's with Sondra and returning to the Cranston's lodge; between waiting for news of the drowning and going on the camping trip; and between staying in the lake region and running away. At Shelter Beach, his instinct is to bolt — yet because of his love for Sondra, he lingers and is captured.

In seeking a confession upon arrest, Mason tells Clyde that only a "sort of fool" would be blind to the overwhelming evidence against him. So bumbling is Clyde that even Mason wonders if such a cold-hearted murderer would forget his gift card in the victim's bag. After his capture, Clyde realizes that leaving the woods so early was a mistake. Too late, he worries about his footprints and other clues. Wincing and chilled, he leans away from Mason. Too late, he knows that he should have destroyed Roberta's and Sondra's letters. Thus weighs the evidence on this "inadequate Atlas."

Inadequate Clyde is a deceiver in a world of deceivers. Although disturbed by Roberta's misidentification at two inns, the coroner conceals the letter to her mother and the contents of her bag until he sees Mason. Titus is flabbergasted to learn of

Roberta's "secret" marriage. Titus considers Clyde to be a city seducer and betrayer, a raper who promised marriage and plotted this terrible crime. Mason reads the letters in Clyde's trunk and discerns the triangle: with a secretly betrayed girl in the background, Clyde Griffiths was ingratiating himself with a girl of a higher social position. On his devious way south from Big Bittern, Clyde follows people from the launch to the train, but slips into a lunchroom with other train passengers. Though troubled by his mistakes, Clyde puts on a genial face at the Cranston's lodge, at the casino, and at the Harriets's. He deceives Sondra into returning to the lodge early, so that he can sink his suit into Twelfth Lake. On Bear Lake, Clyde wears false smiles, and at Ramshorn (where Sondra explains how she has hoodwinked her mother), Clyde evades the truth of Deputy Kraut's questions by outright denials; under Mason's threat of exposure, he nervously distorts the truth.

If clothes do not always reflect a lie, their value is at least relative. Inspecting a mail-order catalog, Coroner Heit wonders how, on his salary, he can buy winter garments for his five children and a fur coat for his wife. Rather than a reflection of glory, clothes to the rumpled Heit are a necessity; his economic condition compels him to weigh the whole political situation: a strong political victory for his friend Mason will reflect on the party and on him. In terms of erotic symbolism, the contrast between innocence and experience is reflected in Sondra's green knitted sports outfit and Roberta's new red silk garters, found in her bag. And to the night hunters, Clyde's city clothes reflect poorly on his integrity; unable to face his friends, Clyde tells the arresting officers that, ironically, his clothes back in camp no longer matter.

Chapters 10-19

This section depicts Clyde Griffiths awaiting trial for murder. With Clyde's tripod and camera discovered, District Attorney Mason presses for action. Samuel Griffiths secures counsel for Clyde; limited by Mr. Griffiths's stipulations (but stimulated by the political situation), Clyde's lawyers plot his defense. Indicted before a special term of the Supreme Court, Clyde is denied a change of venue, and Mason finds further evidence and witnesses. Dreiser achieves the sense of matters coming full circle, back to the gloomy opening of Book I, when the Griffithses of Denver learn of Clyde's imprisonment and Elvira prepares to help Clyde.

In jail, Clyde wishes that someone knew how it all had happened. With hindsight he wishes that he had done certain things differently. Although Roberta's facial injuries were not fatal, autopsy reports indicate that the skull injury "might" have produced death; but, in fact, her water-filled lungs prove that her death was due to drowning. Another causal chain is contemplated by Samuel Griffiths. In retrospect, he sees how alone his nephew was for the first eight months in Lycurgus. But he does not condone Clyde's ungoverned carnality, and he finds it difficult to believe that anyone with Griffiths's "blood" could commit such a crime. Thus he will defend his nephew only if he is innocent. Unable to show insanity in the Griffiths family, Clyde's lawyers nevertheless spin a favorable and plausible web of cause and effect out of the same facts which the district attorney uses to spin an unfavorable and plausible web. Meanwhile Elvira Griffiths, who instructs her grandson Russell in the fundamental verities, traces the cause of Clyde's trouble to the influence of the Green-Davidson and his bad companions there.

To the advantage of his art, Dreiser varies his world of external circumstances. Logical time and cause-effect conventions give way to techniques of simultaneity. The reader witnesses Sondra's reaction and departure to Sharon after Clyde's arrest, and then Clyde's reaction and departure to the Bridgeburg jail. The reader watches Mason develop his case against Clyde as Belknap and Jephson develop their defense for him. Through Elvira Griffiths's stream-of-consciousness (thoughts, plans, biblical quotations), religion and life fuse into a living faith. A symbolic background to the horde of courtroom details is the cold gray October setting, where leaves flying in gusts are like birds; and in the background loom newspaper headlines and the electric chair.

Newspapers not only describe—but print—excerpts from Roberta's letters. These documents result in pity for Roberta and hatred for Clyde. Local newspapers release distorted news. Influence keeps Sondra's letters out of the newspapers and out of the trial itself. Because of their religious and moral beliefs, the Griffithses of Denver exclude daily newspapers from their home and mission. It is Esta, now a suburban Denver wife, who reads the lengthy article about Clyde's indictment in the *Rocky Mountain News*. At his trial Clyde fears what the newspapers will reveal.

As usual, Dreiser's irony is potent. The reactions of the Aldens and the country people contrast with those of the Griffithses and the gentry. The brainy Jephson and the elegant Belknap make effective foils. Ironic also are the implied comparisons between Asa Griffiths and the able and protective fathers of Belknap and Sondra. For the first time in her life, Sondra feels life's grimness. Prior to Clyde's trial, the law, the newspapers, and the crowd already condemn him. The rural community regards him as an outsider, a rich city youth. Finally, to find some peace and quiet, Clyde finds jail a relief. After the autopsy, Mason believes that Clyde struck Roberta with some object and then threw her into the water; Mason is convinced that the deadly object is Clyde's tripod, but later he is convinced that it is Clyde's camera. Although Mason and Heit wonder why they did not discover strands of Roberta's hair in the camera earlier, they accept this new fact as conclusive evidence of Clyde's guilt. Ironically, the public expects the wealthy uncle to defend his nephew, yet criticizes Samuel Griffiths for doing so. Griffiths chooses a Democrat, Belknap, as the ideal lawyer to oppose the Republican, Mason. Again, ironically, Belknap tells Clyde that he will find Jephson as easy to talk to "as you would to your mother." Listening to Clyde's story, Jephson concludes that the truth is too complicated, too unbelievable for a backwoods jury to believe; thus he fabricates a defense and assures Clyde that all will turn out well. Mason, however, finds Clyde's camera before Belknap is even aware that the camera exists.

Learning of Clyde's indictment, the grieving Elvira enters the mission room, where placards proclaim God's charity, wisdom, and righteousness. Although the day of jury selection is cold and windy, the rural crowd evokes a holiday spirit and festival air. Free enterprise has reprinted Roberta's letters in pamphlet form. Clyde sits in his neat gray suit, retrieved from Bear Lake, a counter to Mason's retrieval of the camera. Again, Jephson insists that he will not allow Clyde to be convicted— simply because he is not "allowed to swear to the truth."

In this section Clyde's conviction and eventual electrocution is heavily foreshadowed. The eyes of Clyde's defense lawyer are like a powerful "electric ray." In the county jail Clyde ponders his incredible defense, convinced that the state will electrocute him. In spite of her prayers and actions, Elvira Griffiths soon perceives the strong possibility of her son's electrocution. Meanwhile, Clyde daydreams of various possibilities. At Fourth Lake, Sondra broods about the termination of her girlish fancies. Belknap early imagines Clyde's bewitchment by a rich girl. A victim of a "brainstorm," according to Jephson, Clyde was taken out of himself and made into a different person by the monied class. Yet, despite everything, Clyde has nightmares of the electric chair. He dreams, futilely, of escaping.

Though loyal to Sondra, Clyde has mixed feelings about his attorneys. He is torn between his lawyer's lies and what he knows (or thinks he knows) to be true. Sondra is torn between loyalty to Clyde and loyalty to her position in society. She detests Clyde's crime, yet suffers heartache for him. She hates his past, yet remembers his enthusiasm for her. She wants to see him or send word, yet fears the social reprisals.

From the beginning, some people see Clyde as a weakling. Very early Mason tries to bully him. After four hours of questioning, Samuel Griffiths's attorney views Clyde as possessing a criminality of the most feeble and blundering incapacity. Clyde feels especially worthless when his lawyers discuss his defense as if he were not even in their presence. Belknap commands Clyde not to cry any more—a public confession of guilt. A weak witness, Clyde falls into confusion and fear when the Alden family enters the courtroom.

This section, preparing the way for Clyde's protracted trial, is gorged with deception. Since Clyde lies about his straw hat, Mason sees that he must devise shrewder traps. Before Clyde has legal council, Mason compels Clyde to retrace his steps. On Mason's orders, a deputy ingratiates himself to Clyde, suggesting that to cooperate with Mason is to survive. Still, Clyde denies having a tripod or a camera at the site of the accident. Convinced of Clyde's cold-blooded murder, Burton Burleigh commits a crime himself by tampering with evidence — by twining a few hairs from Roberta's corpse inside the lid of Clyde's camera. Assured of her father's sympathy, Sondra confesses her secret relationship with Clyde. Mason conceals the camera and hairs until the trial which (in view of the political situation) he seeks as soon as possible. Smillie, a Griffiths Company vice president, visits Clyde in jail and detects his lying, but pretends to agree so as not to embarrass him; but Clyde, in turn, detects Smillie's pose. Ironically, Samuel Griffiths wants no chicanery or trickery in the trial. But so weak is Clyde's story that his lawyers concoct another, modified to look less cruel and legally murderous, one designed to gain public sympathy. Also they fake other reasons for Clyde's false confession to Mason. Unable to deny Clyde's two sham registrations and two hats, they play hocus-pocus with Clyde's gray suit (which he wears at the trial). Clyde is in awe of their trickery on his behalf, how they describe his "change of heart." Jephson's defense is that (1) Clyde never plotted murder because he is a moral and physical coward; that (2) Roberta as well as Clyde planned the trip; that (3) Clyde intended to tell Roberta about Sondra; and that (4) he intended to pay Roberta's expenses and then leave town. But after seeing Roberta again and spending two nights with her, Clyde experienced a change of heart: that is, (5) if Roberta still wanted to marry him after he told her about Sondra, Clyde would agree to marry Roberta; that (6) Roberta was indeed willing to marry Clyde; that (7) she jumped up happily, (8) the boat upset, and (9) Clyde struck her accidentally with the camera; that (10) by the time Clyde, a bit dazed himself, could save her, she had drowned; and that (11) because of the suspicious circumstances and his true love for Sondra he (a moral coward) fled to Sondra and her society. The Kansas City accident and Clyde's clandestine affair with Roberta belie other testimony of Clyde's good character. Ironically, Elvira Griffiths (who pretends that Esta's illegitimate son is an adopted orphan in order for Esta to deceive her husband) says that Clyde must not ask her to lie; yet Clyde can tell neither his mother nor his lawyers the truth. Thus to obtain justice (they tell Clyde) they are creating a "fiction" of reality, a translation of the incredible truth into the believable — the improbable into the probable.

Clyde's genuine incarceration, however, reflects on him and on others in striking ways. Despite their disgust for Clyde's crime, his jailers take pride in a Griffiths being in their jail. Meanwhile, the Lycurgus Griffithses think of moving to another city. Recalling Clyde's strange behavior at the lakes, Sondra wants to repossess her letters. Under the name of Wilson, the Finchleys retreat for six weeks to the Maine coast and the Cranstons retreat to the Thousand Islands; those not sufficiently incriminated remain to gossip at Twelfth Lake. While Jephson tries to inoculate Clyde with his shrewdness and courage, Belknap tells Clyde to reflect innocence and to attend Sunday jail services.

Though his sympathetic lawyers are not leaving him stranded, Clyde senses that others are deserting him, or at least qualifying their aid. His uncle makes it clear as to what extent he will help Clyde. That Clyde does not wish to betray Sondra, who forsakes him, amazes his lawyers. Although the lawyers look for someone from Clyde's family to come forward and champion him, the fee-paying Samuel Griffiths does not want the western Griffithses exploited by the press. Clyde's consuming desire is to bolt from jail, to run for his life. More out of curiosity than loyalty, two of Clyde's former society friends appear at the trial; in vain, however, Clyde searches the throng for Sondra.

Chapters 20-26

This section delineates the awesome course of Clyde's trial. Mason blazons his case of Clyde Griffiths as a cold-blooded murderer. Witness after witness steps forward. The trial continues

into November; Mason is elected overwhelmingly to the judgeship. The prosecution concludes with a dramatic reading of
Roberta's letters. Next, Clyde's lawyers construct an elaborate
defense, with Clyde himself as their star witness. In all, one
hundred and twenty-seven witnesses appear in court. Finally,
the jury decides that Clyde is guilty of murder in the first degree.

In terms of literary naturalism, Dreiser attempts to prove
that the mind of a man is directly related to his self-control. In
court Mason asserts that the "mind" foreseeing and forestalling
all of life's accidents indeed is not Clyde's. Clyde marvels at the
unbreakable chain of facts made by various and unexpected witnesses so long after the events. Although Clyde fears death if he
attempts to escape, he views an attempt as at least a chance for
life. In making his defense, Belknap tells the court that Clyde
"happens" to be here because of an incredible and misleading
set of circumstances. Unseemly, Jephson assures Clyde in court
that condemnation can rest *only* on free choice; since Clyde did
not choose to be born, he has no free choice. With regard to his
feelings for Miss X, he was powerless; as for Roberta, he tried to
love her again—but could not.

Through his various narrative techniques, Dreiser balances
psychological and objective detail. Having documented the first
day of the jury selection, the narrator begins this trial section
with this almost stage-like direction: "And then five entire days
consumed by Mason and Belknap in selecting a jury. But at last
the twelve men who were to try Clyde, sworn and seated." The
narrator stresses the hunting, the canine theme by describing
Mason as "a fox hound within the last leap of its kill." Some testimony shocks the reader as well as Clyde—for example, that the
Gilpins knew more regarding Clyde and Roberta than either
suspected, and that the chambermaid at Grass Lake remembered
Clyde's camera and tripod; such withheld information creates
dramatic tension. The signal contrast in this section is the victory
of the prosecution and the defeat of the defense. This defeat is
foreshadowed. When the "electric" prosecutor avers that he will
produce an eye witness to the murder, Clyde grips his chair, his
head jerks back and then drops, and he seems ready to fall into

a coma. As he listens to Mason's artful summation, Clyde is convinced that this jury will convict him.

Clyde's conviction results, for the most part, from Mason's clever use of documents. Mason charges Clyde as a crime-plotter —never writing to Roberta, only sending telephone messages. Of Roberta's letters, Mason first reads (a bit garbled) her last, pathetic threat to Clyde; and then, on the eleventh day, near dusk, Mason slowly and softly reads all of Roberta's letters, crying at certain points and greatly stirring the court. Like Mason, Dreiser achieves strong dramatic effects, for the reader also hears the six letters for the first time. Especially emotional are Roberta's hints of suicide. The newspapers speculate, their sprawling headlines favoring the prosecution; Clyde, thinking of Sondra, mentally answers her questions. The travel folders found in Clyde's bag are almost as crucial as Roberta's letters; even as a witness, Clyde does not detect the Lycurgus House label stamped in red like the red letters of the folder. When, at last, Clyde decides to write a letter, it is only one poignant sentence: "Dear Mother—I am convicted—Clyde." That Roberta's letters convicted him torments Clyde.

Ironically, the jury is convinced of Clyde's guilt even before they sit in judgment. Clyde (the moviegoer) watches Mason in his dynamic role of prosecutor as if someone had shouted: "Lights! Camera!" Mason asserts that Clyde has had more religious, social, and educational advantages than the jurists. As he well knows, Belknap ironically warns the court that it is so easy to distort any set of circumstances. What his lawyers direct him to explain to the jury, Clyde believes: that before meeting Sondra he loved Roberta enormously; ironically, neither Clyde nor the narrator acknowledges the fact that Clyde met Sondra *before* he knew Roberta. Based on the judge's very specific charge, Clyde is *not* guilty of first-degree murder: He struck no intentional blow and the boat capsized accidentally.

Whatever justice is called for, the sensational combination of violence and sex attracts particular attention to Clyde's case. The lawyers draw on their own experiences and temperaments.

While Mason speaks sacredly of sexual union, Belknap focuses on premarital popularity, and Jephson makes innuendoes about extramarital appeal. When Mason declares that Clyde was "intimate" with Miss Alden while pursuing Miss X, the rural folk crane forward. Realizing how shabby his sexual life must appear, Clyde also feels that it is not too unusual, at least by the standards of some of Lycurgus society.

Despite Clyde's struggling to believe in himself, his sense of inferiority overwhelms him. Committed to perjury, Clyde is a deficient witness. He twists, swallows stigmatically, and sinks in his chair. He feels weak, nervous, and false, and his nerves fail after Mason asks why he did not simply push the boat to the struggling Roberta. When Mason asserts that Clyde wanted Roberta to drown, Clyde cowers in his seat. When Mason dramatically shows him a lock of Roberta's hair, he shrinks back. He is determined not to let Mason bully him, but he feels weak and unable to draw strength from Jephson's eyes. In answer to his partner's soothing contention that the uncourageous Clyde had the best possible defense, Jephson counters with his soothing belief that Clyde really did kill Roberta.

From the beginning, Dreiser illuminates the elusiveness of truth. Trapping Clyde in little lies, Mason hopes to discredit the explanation of a change of heart. (Clyde never admits to his own lawyers that he did not wish to save Roberta.) On the stand, Clyde testifies that (1) he never plotted to kill Roberta, that (2) she wanted to go to the lakes, that (3) he procured the tourist folders in Utica, that (4) he falsely registered to avoid scandal, that (5) he bought another hat because his was soiled, that (6) he had a change of heart about deserting Roberta, that (7) he carried his bag only because he had a lunch in it, that (8) Roberta jumped up with joy in the boat upon his agreeing to marry her, that (9) he tried to catch her with his camera in hand, that (10) being dazed, he called to her to catch onto the drifting boat, that (11) after Roberta drowned he thought *for the first time* that others might think he also had drowned, that (12) he knew nothing about his missing hat lining, that (13) he asked the hunters for directions — not distances — and that (14) he did ask the price of boat rentals on Big Bittern. In the end, Clyde swears that the drowning was an accident (indeed, it all *had not been precisely* as he had planned).

Belknap speaks of Clyde's actions as a result of an intense conflict between two illicit moods. During the trial Clyde's courage ebbs and flows. Mason's threat of a witness shocks Clyde into picturing the truth for himself: (1) the unintended blow, (2) the boat's upsetting, (3) Roberta's cries for help, (4) his passivity, (5) his swimming to shore, (6) his changing clothes, and (7) his flight. Downhearted after Mason's dynamic presentation, Clyde is heartened by Belknap's opening defense. To distract the jury from the charge of murder, Jephson attacks the defendant as a moral coward. Hesitating and stumbling through his memorized answers, Clyde shows himself a weakling, incapable—Jephson hopes to prove—of murder. Belknap explains that Clyde hesitated fatally but not criminally, the one time in his life when he should not have hesitated. And in his summation, Belknap refers to Clyde's "dreamy mind." At the trial Clyde is both participant and spectator. Although Jephson rhetorically alludes to *The Arabian Nights,* Clyde's bewitchment by beauty, love, and wealth is in the deepest sense true. His dream-love remains an unrealized ideal. After the verdict Clyde visualizes the ghostly electric chair looming ever closer.

Chapters 27-34

This section documents Clyde's confinement in the state penitentiary and his execution. Through her newspaper articles and public appearances, Elvira Griffiths fights for appeal money. Meanwhile, Asa becomes ill in Denver; in a burst of sympathy Clyde's lawyers advise Elvira to return home while they appeal Clyde's case. From Denver, Elvira pleads with the Reverend Duncan McMillan to save Clyde's soul. All appeals fail. Clyde dies in the electric chair. Asa and Elvira Griffiths, with their grandson, Russell, carry on their religious work.

The end is a natural and inevitable consequence of all that has happened. Like Clyde, the other prisoners have (according to Dreiser) responded to some "chemistry" of their natures or circumstances. Death here is ushered in by men crying, praying, losing their minds, yet the terrifying process continues. Vividly, Dreiser describes Clyde's mind as he realizes that he himself waits in a cell where others have waited before him and will wait after him. Thinking how differently his life now would be had he listened to his mother's teachings, Clyde knows how difficult it would be to overcome his impulses and desires. Even after confessing his guilt, Clyde rebels against his judges, for no one — not even his mother — has experienced his particular suffering. Locked within himself and in an iron, mechanical system, Clyde dreams of his end — and so it is: guards push him through a little door, the door quickly closes, and there is no return.

In this final powerful climax, Dreiser uses all of his art and craft as a novelist. After the trial Elvira Griffiths's tractarian faith contrasts with the journalists's skepticism and her brother-in-law's detachment. Clyde's colorful journey over hills and fields contrasts with his confinement behind penitentiary walls. Dreiser details the Dantesque Death House — its white narrow hard walls, iron bars, harsh incandescent light, its horrible food, its lack of privacy, and its groans and screams of despair. For all its sordid detail, the Death House is also a moral setting, with the narrator acting as pathologist for a diseased social system. In exposé style he indicts society's Death House as a place of unnecessary and unauthorized cruelty, of stupid and destructive torture, a place where a criminal suffers a thousand deaths before the one to which he is sentenced. The narrator sketches Clyde's mates on murderer's row — most of them coarse, stupid, or sinister. A symbolist manqué, Dreiser reveals how Clyde now sees the horned beast of his jungle nightmares as the flashing electric chair. In an effective shift of focus, the unswayed governor looks out on the death image of a snowy February landscape. The traumatic aftermath of Clyde's electrocution comes to the reader not through the narrator's typical blunt slicing of chronology, but through the horrified recreation of the death scene in the delicate mind of the Reverend Duncan McMillan.

Until the end, Dreiser's novel has documentary appeal, in itself and in its use of documents. Unlike Clyde, Elvira Griffiths, as a crusading mother and correspondent, gets a good press, but in time Clyde's notoriety wanes. Nicholson, the condemned ex-lawyer, advises Clyde that in the event of another trial only a digest of the facts in Roberta's letters (not the emotional letters themselves) should be admitted as evidence. Sondra's unsigned typewritten note is alien to her early inanities. After destroying his own letters, the refined Nicholson leaves Clyde his copies of *Robinson Crusoe* and *The Arabian Nights*—titles symbolic of Clyde's being a solitary dreamer and a beached fantast. However, the central document in Clyde's life becomes the Holy Bible, from which McMillan quotes freely. Clyde's letter of Christian victory seems almost as hollow and mechanical as Elvira's last reply from the governor's office.

Dreiser's pattern of irony pushes toward his circular conclusion. To escape publicity, the suffering Griffithses of Denver move, but their address is revealed by the van company. In aiding Elvira, the reporters and newspapers also exploit her, as Samuel Griffiths expected. He himself is sorry that, out of sentiment, he ever involved himself with Clyde. Like the western Griffithses, so now the eastern Griffithses, reflecting notoriety, move because of their status and their children. Ironically, Elvira thinks that the newspapers (the source for Clyde's murderous plot) might help save him. Clyde, who aspired to wear fashionable clothes (and did to some extent), is in a cell across from a sinister Oriental, dressed like himself. In addition, Nicholson's cool factualism is an ironic contrast to the fervent imagination of the Reverend McMillan, whose sympathy for Roberta and her family embraces Clyde and his family. And whereas Nicholson would appeal to the secular, McMillan would appeal to the divine. Pondering his case, Clyde wonders if his false form of defense is in itself sufficiently mitigating to warrant an appeal. Furthermore, if he is now truly contrite, fit for life and action, the state's killing him compounds crime with crime. Out of his need for sympathy, yearning, and deliverance, Clyde confides more in McMillan than in his mother; from McMillan's manner, Elvira fears that Clyde is guilty. Although Clyde declares his Christian conversion, true to his own nature he seems to backslide onto the island of himself, where (like Robinson Crusoe) he must try to construct his own consolation. In the end, Clyde is only numb and bewildered. After Clyde's execution, the tormented McMillan begins to doubt the quality of his own mercy and wisdom; by extension, has he, in fact, merely stood by, watching Clyde drown?

Clyde's electrocution—so early hinted at—is oppressively anticipated in this section. The anonymous voice asking a guard if there is any word from Albany is Clyde's last hope. The narrational reference to sundry clergymen who visit amenable prisoners on "murderer's row" prefigures the appearance of the Reverend Duncan McMillan. Clyde's electrocution itself simply repeats for the last time all the other executions of his nightmares.

Thus, in the end, nightmare and reality, coming ever closer, finally fuse. Until this time Clyde's imagination has been habitually at odds with causal action. Even in the Death House, Clyde is drawn more to life-as-it-might-be than to life-as-it-is. He reads light romantic novels which picture ideal worlds. Though still smouldering, Clyde sees the fever of his former life as a form of insanity, and as he reads Sondra's unsigned note in the dusk, the last trace of his vain, impossible dream vanishes. After the court's denial, the Reverend McMillan assures Clyde that only the next world, not this one, is important. Clyde fails to make his mother understand his dream of success—the American Dream which Dreiser depicts as vulgar and as tragic because of its often deadly consequences. Despite McMillan's assurance of Paradise, when Clyde shuffles toward the final door he sees only the dreaded chair of his nightmares.

Until these last moments, Dreiser documents Clyde's internal torments. Clyde both dreads and desires to see his mother. Wincing to learn that she will hear his sentence, he knows, too, that his future depends on her efforts alone. Clyde's dubious manner in jail chills Elvira. Divided now herself, she prays for belief in her son. Wanting to repent, Clyde nevertheless feels it expedient to wait until the court of appeal reaches a decision. When Clyde confesses to McMillan, he realizes his own complicated emotions in the boat—pity, shame, anger, hate, and fear. Puzzled, McMillan tries to follow Clyde's agonized thoughts. Seeking exactitude, splitting hairs, struggling to translate recollected emotions, Clyde pits (as is his habit) one idea against another. But when Clyde admits to thinking that if Roberta drowned he would be free to wed Sondra, McMillan declares: "In your heart was murder then." Although he overtly agrees with McMillan, Clyde is still bewildered by McMillan's seeming power to make clear the ambiguity of reality.

In the Death House, Clyde experiences the extremes of feeling superior and inferior, yet even here he is courteous and tactful. The "Chinaman" across his cell horrifies him and he wonders if the brute murderers here will cause him trouble. An outsider (even here), Clyde is full of self-pity, for no one sympathizes with his wretchedness. He becomes sick when he listens to the hungry inmates eat—like animals, growling and scraping. Their insanity terrifies him. But numb and dumb, unable to think or even cry after witnessing his first ritual of death, he shivers and shakes. And unlike Nicholson on his own day of death, Clyde is sick and feverish.

But even in jail he strains to deceive his mother. Telling her about his not intending to strike Roberta, he lies nervously about his intention to let the girl drown. To give his mother some comfort, he conceals how execrable is the Death House; and he never tells her all that he has confessed to McMillan. Believing that Clyde is guilty before God and Caesar, McMillan, as Clyde's spiritual advisor, will not lie for him—for by forsaking Clyde here, he saves him for the hereafter.

In the shadow of death, Clyde realizes that his mother, at least, did not desert him. In turn, Elvira believes that in her need, God will not forsake her. But she cannot abandon her husband to aid Clyde alone.

Clyde wonders how different his life might have been had his lust for women and wealth been less fierce; he wonders if religious persons have inferior passions or superior courage. As one who has heard many confessions, Elvira knows the many moods of consent and the methods of allurement, the temptations which her son did not resist. Although McMillan does not see adultery as tantamount to murder, his own sexuality is repressed or sublimated. Even the governor (says the narrator) has never felt Clyde's fevers and fires.

To be sure, the stress of impending death dislocates Clyde's former love of fine clothes. No longer are his mother's shabby brown coat and ridiculous brown hat so disturbing. In contrast to his once expensive suits and hats, Number 77221 now wears a striped uniform and a hideous cap. No mirror in his cell reflects this indignity. In his final hour Clyde is furnished felt slippers, gray socks, black trousers, and — irony of ironies — a white shirt *without a collar.*

Throughout *An American Tragedy,* Dreiser has dramatized the failure of religion to guide Clyde over the hazardous terrain of modern American life. Nowhere is this failure more dramatized than in this section. The narrator's picture of Elvira praying in her dreary mission is that of a biblical figure as an alien in a six-thousand-year-old world. As Elvira prays for help, she thinks of the newspapers and thanks God for this enlightenment. Even some skeptics are moved by her earnestness, faith, and love. The pragmatic Jephson thinks that the religious element which was ready to condemn Clyde might now aid his mother — and Elvira views this as the voice and hand of God. Fighting fiendish doubts about Clyde and about God's desertion, she reaffirms her faith and encourages Clyde to read specific pages from the Bible. Ironically, the prevailing attitude among the professed Christians is that the shabbiness of the unordained Elvira Griffiths reflects on established sects, that her evangelism has directed her attention away from her growing son, and that a church is no place to debate her son's case. The narrator depicts Christian futility further in Pasquale's insanity: crawling around his cell, he mumbles prayers, taps his forehead on the floor, kisses it, and licks the feet of a brass Christ. Out of fear or contrition, others fall on their knees. After Pasquale's electrocution, Clyde's only reaction is: "God! God! God! God!" Assuring the warden that he has come for the sake of Clyde's mother and Clyde's soul,

McMillan prays immediately. Out of his isolation, out of a past, present, and future too painful to contemplate, Clyde yields himself to McMillan's friendship and interest. After his lengthy confession, Clyde broods on its effect on McMillan, while McMillan sees Clyde as filled with God's spirit. Elvira accepts McMillan's word of Clyde's salvation. But still clutching at contrition, Clyde wonders how one can do without sun, rain, work, love, energy, and desire. In short, Clyde does not want to die, and he cannot understand why McMillan did not lie to save him. Clyde prays to God to let him live, but is dubious about the quality of his newfound peace. After Clyde's death, doubts assail McMillan; but, strong in her faith, Elvira Griffiths prays for the soul of her son and tries to visualize him in the arms of his Maker.

With slight variations, the "Souvenir" section repeats the novel's opening section, showing the continuing nature of the social tragedy. A shabby band of five—Asa, Elvira, Russell, and a mother and daughter—preach and sing in the streets of San Francisco. Through the dense metallic world a determined Elvira leads her Bible-and-hymnal-carrying grandson, the object of pedestrian sympathy. The narrator paints the same pathetic tract-counting (sixteen fewer taken than in the parallel opening scene), the dreary mission, and the ironic mottoes. Elvira Griffiths's fighting faith in God's love and justice seems beyond comprehension, beyond this tragic life. But for Clyde's sake, she gives Russell (who resembles his dead uncle) a dime for drugstore ice cream. As the four believers disappear behind the yellow door, Dreiser's somber narrator notes that the characters "disappeared."

CHARACTER ANALYSES

CLYDE GRIFFITHS

Dreiser's protagonist-victim lusts after the American Dream of Success. He is disposed to the acquisition of material wealth in order to buy expensive clothes, to be chauffeured around in handsome automobiles, and to dine in luxurious restaurants. He yearns for amorous adventures, both erotic and romantic. He trusts in adventurous companions, pleasure seekers like himself who indulge in parties, brightly lit and full of music. And, finally, he deems personal freedom and independence of utmost importance, as a way to escape pain, responsibility, restraint, and family.

Throughout his short life Clyde has seen his family's narrow reliance on prayer and precept bring no success, only trouble. His resigned father, unlike his rich uncle, is a failure. Clyde loathes his family's poverty and ignorance, their inability to help him and to give him the things he craves. He resents his parents's embarrassing religious labors in dreary mission houses and on city streets. Their rootlessness has contributed to his irregular education and to his sense of feeling always an outsider.

Thwarted by his sordid environment and impelled by his emotionalism and exotic sense of romance inherited from his father, the lonely Clyde daydreams of success. Outside the mission world his response to certain physical forms — clothes, girls, lighted residences — is strong. Into them he projects his envy, lust, and melancholy. Though eager for pleasure, yet he reasons about its adverse consequences. But since he is by nature weak, he intuits that for good or bad, powerful forces within and without overwhelm him. Defeated by temptation, he instinctively rationalizes, and his reward is a renewed sense of his own glory and worth.

Underlying Clyde's progress from low- to middle- to high-class life is a weak, sometimes vicious, morality. From the beginning, the handsome Clyde Griffiths is characterized as nervously refined. As a bellhop he learns to ingratiate himself with different kinds of people and to adjust to the social cannibalism around him. Although outwardly respectful, he remains aloof from vulgarians both below and equal to his station. He cloaks his poor origins, secret indulgences, and suspect behavior in evasions and outright lying. His instinct to flee from obligations and accidents transforms his mental and moral cowardice into mental and "accidental" murder.

In the Death House he turns to his mother and to Reverend McMillan, trying to find the God he never believed in. So patient and sincere is McMillan that Clyde pours out his confession and achieves a sense of relief and belief. But with no hope for a stay of execution, Clyde falls into doubt. Though McMillan promises him salvation, Number 77221 senses very little as he shuffles to the electric chair. Ironically, Clyde Griffiths seems reincarnated in the pathetic little figure of his nephew, Russell.

ELVIRA GRIFFITHS

Clyde's mother believes in a merciful God Almighty. She believes also that through her faith and good works she has been called upon to spread the word of God. Though preoccupied with saving souls, she deeply loves her children, knowing full well that they carry the weaknesses and sins of all mankind. Shabbily dressed and housed, she believes in struggling and suffering for the glory of God and salvation, not for vanity and material gain. So possessed is she by spiritual fervor that she is unable to comprehend the degree of Clyde's secular dreams.

Her own dreams began to form after she fell in love with the visionary Asa Griffiths. As an ignorant farm girl she had given little thought to religion. But inoculated by the "virus" of evangelism, she joined in her husband's religious adventures to illusory greener fields. Before Kansas City, Denver, and San Francisco, the Griffithses had conducted missions or preached in the streets of Grand Rapids, Detroit, Milwaukee, Quincy, and Chicago. Like her husband, Elvira is ignorant of their children's need for practical or professional training.

In spite of her pains, this extreme Protestant remains optimistic. She tries to solve family problems and professional difficulties through her prayers. Sublimating her own drives, Elvira views the physical world as the devil's playground, where evil delights tempt the innocent and the unwary. She intuits an eternal afterlife. Yet when her maternal instinct is aroused, she yearns to save her children from disgrace and death.

Her motives in trying to save Esta and Clyde are good, but Clyde's need tests her resources to the limit, especially since she doubts his truthfulness. In an effort to save him, she exposes herself to the glare of publicity and to the stings of ridicule. Although she fails to save Clyde's life, she benefits Esta. By her courageous act of adopting Esta's illegitimate child, however, she brings upon herself the torment of living a lie.

Still believing in a beneficent Deity, she prays for the salvation of Clyde's soul. In fact, her faith is not only intact but stronger because of her suffering. Elvira comes to sense the powerful influence of the Green-Davidson, the pleasure-seeking companions, fugitiveness, sexual temptation, and high society on her weak son. She also realizes how little she helped Clyde prepare for life in this world. For his sake, she gives her grandson Russell a dime for ice cream.

SAMUEL GRIFFITHS

Clyde's uncle, the owner of Griffiths Collar and Shirt Company in Lycurgus, New York, personifies the American Dream realized. He places great value on his good name, his family, his wealth, his possessions, and his status. He also believes that working hard develops character, especially for those destined to rise. His attitudes and beliefs seem close to those which Benjamin Franklin expressed in his *Autobiography*.

Clyde's fortunate uncle is a foil to Clyde's unfortunate father, whom Samuel Griffiths has not seen in thirty years. Back in Bertwick, Vermont, Joseph Griffiths willed his property to his three sons—one thousand dollars to the "mushy" Asa and some fifteen thousand dollars each to Samuel and another son. The chosen Samuel invested his money in the Lycurgus factory. In time, his family became esteemed in the region, if not among the oldest families, then among the most conservative, respectable, and successful. Until Clyde arrived in Lycurgus, nothing had happened to weather or darken its prestige.

Sensing the injustice done to Asa, the incisive Samuel Griffiths wants to help his well-mannered nephew in some way. Then, too, as an affectionate family man, he is moved by the remarkable physical resemblance between his young blood relative and his own son. Cautious by nature, the economic necessitarian yields to sentimental nepotism. But he yields only in his logical framework of conditions and stipulations. And for all his commercial shrewdness, he does not detect as quickly as do his wife and youngest daughter the depths of Gilbert's resentment toward his western cousin.

When his nephew is arrested and charged with murder, the calm and judicious Samuel Griffiths puts a premium on the morality of the golden mean. Generously he provides legal counsel, but with numerous conditions and qualifications. These qualifications rise out of his vanity, family pride, and enlightened self-interest. Most important, he will retain lawyers for Clyde only if they are honest and if Clyde is innocent. Thus in good faith he has invited Clyde to Lycurgus, provided him with a job, with social invitations, and with defense attorneys, but in each instance only up to a point.

After Clyde is judged guilty of murder, Samuel Griffiths does what he must to protect himself, his business, and his family. Indeed, something has happened now to darken his and his family's prestige, and perhaps he and his family have contributed to this. Too disgraced to stay in Lycurgus, he and Gilbert decide to relocate the business in South Boston and the family in one of the suburbs, or elsewhere. Macerated by the course of events, Samuel convinces himself that Asa's treatment by their father, after all, was not unfair. Finally, he regretfully abandons Clyde and rededicates himself to the rule that sentiment in business is folly.

ROBERTA ALDEN

Clyde's factory girl friend believes in life and love. Like Clyde, she desires a better life and better marriage prospects, but she has no grand illusions about marrying into wealth and luxury. She believes in the efficacy of her efforts and in the value of continuing her education. Morality is important to her, but the power of eros overwhelms her. Before her death she settles for the facade of respectability.

Like Elvira, Roberta is the daughter of a poor farmer. Her family's poverty forces her to work in a nearby factory. Although her looks, charm, and morals are superior to those of her rural community, the suitable young men there identify her as a "factory type." Her knowledge of men and of birth control are very limited.

Her shyness stems, in large part, from feelings of inferiority, a legacy of her early factory days. She is attracted not only to Clyde's charm and position, but to his physical attributes. Her response to nature is sensuous and serene when she picks water lilies and when she trails a hand in the lake. Passionately loving Clyde, she afterwards feels guilty, but continues the affair. Despair turns to hope after Clyde agrees to marry her.

Breaking the social taboo by chatting with the foreign girls at the factory, Roberta also breaks a factory taboo by meeting with her supervisor. She not only meets Clyde secretly, but violates her sexual code. For Clyde's sake (and to not disgrace her family) she seeks an abortion and, failing that, contemplates suicide. Behind her is a trail of evasion and deception. In a last effort to save herself and her family's respectability, she threatens Clyde into a temporary marriage, knowing that he is indifferent to her.

Roberta's corpse is the object of the district attorney's powerful sympathies. From her head, Burton Burleigh ghoulishly snatches a few hairs with which to incriminate Clyde. At the trial Mason thrusts upon Clyde a long light brown lock of his "dead love's hair." Newspapermen, pamphleteers, and the prosecuting attorney exploit Roberta's pathetic letters. And, through Mason, the court hears her speak, as if from the grave.

SONDRA FINCHLEY

Those material things which cause Clyde to contemplate murder are taken for granted by his American Dream Girl. Typifying young, sophisticated wealth, Sondra Finchley is the glass of Lycurgus fashion. She is devoted to clothes and fun and games and romantic love. Society is her stage and nature is her playground. She plays with the conventions around her but does not break them.

Unlike Roberta Alden, Sondra Finchley is the daughter of a rich manufacturer. She is not only popular with her select social circle, but she is its pace-setter. Her pursuits—swimming, boating, riding, driving, tennis, and golf—seem more like outdoor parties. And at parties it is her custom to shatter young men with her charms, Gilbert Griffiths excepted. In spite of the demands upon her attentions, she remains very much her own young lady, free of entangling alliances or compromises.

But so supreme is Clyde's adulation of her that this "seeking Aphrodite" becomes infatuated with her worshipper. Cautious and doubtful, she is puzzled by the chemistry of mutual attraction. Dreiser's treatment of her "Clyde-Mydie" love patter and love letters is deeply satiric. Though intellectually shallow, Sondra is clever, her mind quick and inventive. At Twelfth Lake she thinks what a great lark it would be to elope with Clyde, but her ingrained sense of the practical reconciles the best of both worlds—until Clyde's arrest.

In the beginning, Sondra's interest in Clyde is not real, only a device to irritate Gilbert Griffiths. Furthermore, if harm seems headed her way, she plans to drop Clyde quickly. To deceive both Gilbert and her parents, Sondra uses her friends as "fronts" to Clyde's entrance into her set. Once in, Clyde is the object of her pretended indifference, her teasing, and her flirting. Feeling herself drawn toward him, she nevertheless keeps him as behaved and leashed as her French bulldog, Bissell, by impressing him with luxuries, by handing him money on the sly, by warning him of her parents's disapproval, and by conjuring up a picture of matrimonial and executive bliss.

Known only as "Miss X" during Clyde's trial, and still shielded by her father's influence and wealth, Sondra retreats to Narragansett. Having seen life's grimness for the first time in her young life, she broods on the loss of her girlhood innocence. She longs to repossess her letters to Clyde. Yet she writes Clyde one last note – typewritten, anonymous, and in the third person. When Clyde reads of her remembrance, suffering, bewilderment, sorrow, sympathy, and good wishes, the last trace of his golden dream vanishes.

ORVILLE W. MASON

Even during Clyde Griffiths's trial, the short, broad-chested, dynamic district attorney of Cataraqui County seems well on his way toward realizing the American Dream. On the make, he struggles for success in the form of additional political and legal power. Eager for victory and fame, he believes in seizing the main chance. Knowing that the strong more often than not crush the weak, Mason is determined to be strong. Certainly he means to conquer those whose boyhoods were less toilsome than his.

Like Clyde, Mason's early poverty and neglect serve as a spur to his ambition. The son of a poor farmer, he early set aside childish things and helped his widowed mother. At seventeen, he began reporting for newspapers in the region, and at nineteen began law studies in the Bridgeburg office of a former judge. After a few years in state politics he returned to Bridgeburg as assistant district attorney, auditor, and then district attorney for two terms. Married (to the daughter of the local druggist) and the father of two children, Mason sees in Clyde's case the answer to the problem of his political future.

Another spur to Mason's ambition is his sinister-looking broken nose, disfigured as the result of a skating accident in his youth. Although Mason is a type of the Dreiserian superman, he is also rather romantic and emotional. He is sensitive about his facial handicap — "what the Freudians are accustomed to describe as a psychic sex scar." The reader is to understand that significant connections exist between Mason's repressed sexuality, his commiseration for the dead Roberta, and his bias against handsome, wealthy young men. In the light of his gallant sympathy and political ambition, Mason shrewdly, energetically, and boldly defends the lovely dead girl who can neither defend herself nor rebuff her broken-nosed champion.

To prosecute Clyde, the articulate and energetic Mason acts out of not altogether virtuous motives. His primary intention is neither to find the truth nor to achieve justice, but to get himself elected to a judgeship. Although he courageously commits himself to victory, he has much support, both honest and dishonest. Ruthlessly he hurts Clyde, to the benefit of himself, his friends, and his party.

His combative instincts aroused by community support and a faltering defendant, Mason is pictured as a foxhound leaping at its prey. Bullying, sarcastic, and sly, Mason affects oratorical displays which enhance his instinct to dominate a scene. Even before the trial ends, the voters sweep him into office. He continues to pile fact upon fact, witness upon witness, and he introduces mathematical demonstration and physical evidence, including a boat and two small hairs. In the end, Clyde's nemesis, Roberta's avenger, walks royally out of court with his entourage, a conquering hero amid the cheering herd of men.

REVIEW QUESTIONS AND ESSAY TOPICS

1. Was Clyde Griffiths guilty of murder in the first degree?

2. Discuss the American city as a symbol of twentieth-century materialism.

3. Compare the attitudes of Mason, Burleigh, Heit, Belknap, and Jephson toward the law.

4. Discuss the irony of Clyde Griffiths as a dreamer.

5. How does Dreiser as omniscient narrator deal with the physico-chemical view of man?

6. Discuss Dreiser's variations on clock time.

7. What is the meaning of Clyde's several nightmares?

8. What is the relationship between Clyde's differing views of Roberta and Sondra?

9. Describe the role of Asa Griffiths in terms of the narrative. Is his effect on Clyde more or less significant than that of his wife?

10. How do films influence Clyde?

11. Does Clyde change during the long course of this novel?

12. How does the Reverend McMillan contribute to Clyde's death?

13. Discuss the east-west theme in *An American Tragedy*.

14. How does Hortense fail Clyde? How does Rita? Roberta? Sondra?

15. Analyze Dreiser's style. What are its strong and weak points?

16. With respect to probability, how does Dreiser establish the likelihood of events occurring which would be most unlikely in ordinary life? Which would be likely in ordinary life but not in fiction?

17. How does *An American Tragedy* achieve its greatest moments of tension?

18. What are the advantages and the disadvantages of Dreiser's omniscient point of view?

19. How does Dreiser attempt to individualize speech? How successful is he?

20. What social problems does Dreiser regard as unsolved? Have they been solved since 1925?

21. Discuss the regional aspects of Dreiser's novel. Discuss its universal aspects.

22. What is Dreiser's attitude or the attitude of the "implied author" toward the idea of moral purpose in the universe?

SELECTED BIBLIOGRAPHY

ELIAS, ROBERT H. *Theodore Dreiser: Apostle of Nature.* New York: Alfred A. Knopf, Inc. 1949. Best single scholarly book on Dreiser.

FROHOCK, W. M. *Theodore Dreiser.* Minneapolis: University of Minnesota Press, 1970. Pamphlet in American Writers Series, 102. Lucid sketch of life and work.

GERBER, PHILLIP L. *Theodore Dreiser.* New York: Twayne Publishers, Inc., 1964. Twayne's United States Authors Series, 52. Crisp overview of Dreiser's career and works.

KAZIN, ALFRED and CHARLES SHAPIRO. (eds.) *The Stature of Theodore Dreiser.* Bloomington: Indiana University Press, 1955. Collects best Dreiser criticism between 1900 and 1955.

LEHAN, RICHARD. *Theodore Dreiser, His World and His Novels.* Carbondale: Southern Illinois University Press, 1969. Integrates Dreiser's art and life.

MATTHIESSEN, F. O. *Theodore Dreiser.* New York: William Sloan Associates, Inc., 1951. A fine critical biography.

MOERS, ELLEN. *Two Dreisers.* New York: Viking Press, 1969. Excellent on Dreiser's novelistic art.

SALZMAN, JACK. *The Merrill Studies in* "An American Tragedy." Columbia: Charles E. Merrill Publishing Company, 1971. Thirteen important reviews and studies.

WARREN, ROBERT PENN. *Homage to Theodore Dreiser.* New York: Random House, 1971. Analyzes Dreiser's art and the problem of Clyde's identity.

NOTES

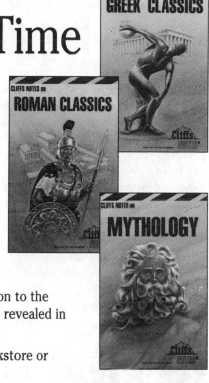